To:
....
....

From:
....
....

Try these tasty:
....
....

Date made:
....

Ingredients:
....
....

Baked for you with love from:

....

Try these tasty:

....
....

Date made:

....

Ingredients:

....
....

To:

....

....

From:

....

....

Try these tasty:

....

....

Date made:

....

Ingredients:

....

....

Baked for you with love from:

....

Try these tasty:
....
....
Date made:
....
Ingredients:
....
....

To:
....
....
From:
....
....

Try these tasty:
....
....
Date made:
....
Ingredients:
....
....

Baked for you with love from:

....

Try these tasty:

....
....

Date made:

....

Ingredients:

....
....

To: ....
....

From: ....
....

Try these tasty:
....
....

Date made: ....
....

Ingredients: ....
....

Baked for you with love from:

....

Try these tasty:

....
....

Date made:

....

Ingredients:

....
....

Cookie Jar

Cookie Jar

80 recipes for irresistible
home-baked cookies

First published in 2011
LOVE FOOD is an imprint of Parragon Books Ltd

Parragon
Queen Street House
4 Queen Street
Bath BA1 1HE, UK

ISBN: 978-1-4454-2879-6

Printed in China

Cover design by Talking Design
Introduction by Fiona Biggs

Notes for the Reader
This book uses both metric and imperial measurements. Follow the same units of measurement throughout; do not mix metric and imperial. All spoon measurements are level: teaspoons are assumed to be 5 ml, and tablespoons are assumed to be 15 ml. Unless otherwise stated, milk is assumed to be full fat, eggs and individual vegetables are medium, and pepper is freshly ground black pepper.

The times given are an approximate guide only. Preparation times differ according to the techniques used by different people and the cooking times may also vary from those given. Optional ingredients, variations or serving suggestions have not been included in the calculations.

Recipes using raw or very lightly cooked eggs should be avoided by infants, the elderly, pregnant women, convalescents and anyone suffering from an illness. Pregnant and breastfeeding women are advised to avoid eating peanuts and peanut products. Sufferers from nut allergies should be aware that some of the ready-made ingredients used in the recipes in this book may contain nuts. Always check the packaging before use.

CONTENTS

Introduction	6
Classic Favourites	8
Chocolate Choice	50
Fabulous Fruit & Nut	92
Something Special	134
Index	176
Gift Labels	177

INTRODUCTION

There's nothing quite as enticing as the tantalizing aroma of freshly baked cookies. As soon as you bite into a moist, warm home-baked cookie, you realize just how delicious and moreish they are. Cookies are very easy to make, are tastier than the shop-bought variety and, with no artificial flavourings, preservatives or hydrogenated fats, are much healthier too.

They are also a great way to get children involved in cooking with you – little ones just love cutting out their favourite shapes and icing their baked creations.

Once you get the cookie bug, you'll always be keen to bake a fresh batch so that you can try out a variety of ingredients. These treats are ideal for lunchboxes, for friends dropping in for coffee or for children to enjoy with a glass of milk when they get back from school. When stored in an airtight container, cookies keep for longer than cakes and so are practical, as well as tasty!

Packaged attractively, a batch of home-made cookies is the perfect gift when visiting family and friends or for donating to a bake sale at a fête or at work. The gift labels at the back of this book will add a lovely personal touch to your baked goods. Pack the cookies in an airtight jar, crisp cellophane bag or an attractive box or tin, then simply cut out a label, fill in the details and attach it to the container with a length of pretty ribbon tied in a bow.

Making Cookies

Whether you're an experienced cook or a novice baker, following a few simple rules will give you perfect cookies every time:

- Before you start to cook, read the recipe all the way through carefully. Gather all the ingredients together and weigh them accurately.
- Preheat the oven to the required temperature.
- Do any chopping, slicing or grating of the ingredients before you start mixing them.
- Don't take shortcuts – if the recipe asks you to chill the dough prior to cutting, do so, as the dough will be easier to cut and the baked cookies will have a better finish.
- When making drop cookies, leave enough space to allow for expansion during cooking, otherwise you'll end up with one large cookie!
- Freshly-baked cookies are very soft when just baked, so leave them to cool slightly on the baking sheet before transferring them to a wire rack to cool completely.

Always store cookies in an airtight container, separate from cakes – cookies will absorb the moisture from cakes, leaving you with soggy cookies and dried-out cakes!

When making cookie dough you can always double up on the quantities and freeze any that you don't need. This is a great way to avoid a last-minute rush on festive occasions, when you might want to make large batches of cookies as gifts. Wrap the dough tightly in clingfilm and chill in the refrigerator, before placing in a freezer bag and transferring to the freezer. Drop cookies can be frozen on baking sheets, then placed in freezer bags and transferred to the freezer. Cookie dough will keep well in the freezer for 4–6 weeks. When you remove the dough from the freezer, leave to stand at room temperature for 30 minutes before baking.

Equipment

You don't need a lot of equipment for preparing and baking cookies, but do make sure that you have the following basic tools:

- Kitchen scales and/or measuring jug and spoons
- Some wooden spoons for mixing
- A rolling pin for rolling out the cookie dough
- A saucepan for melting butter (although you can also do this in a bowl in the microwave oven)
- A heavy baking sheet
- Cookie cutters in different shapes and sizes
- A spatula or palette knife for lifting the cookies off the baking sheet
- A wire rack

Storecupboard

You will need to check your storecupboard regularly to keep an eye on use-by dates, as some storecupboard ingredients deteriorate quickly. Staples might include:

- Seeds – sesame, poppy, sunflower and pumpkin
- Nuts – almonds, walnuts, hazelnuts and pine kernels
- Dried fruit and berries – raisins, sultanas, currants, apricots, cranberries, mangoes and figs
- Spices – cinnamon, ginger, nutmeg and vanilla extract
- Chocolate and chocolate chips – white, milk and plain
- Sugar – granulated, caster, demerara and soft brown. Granulated sugar will give a crunchier texture than caster sugar.
- Flour – plain white and plain wholemeal. Cookies baked with wholemeal flour will have extra fibre, a nutty flavour and a denser texture.

One of the great things about baking cookies is that you don't have to stick rigidly to all of the ingredients specified. You can usually make some substitutions – walnuts for almonds, cranberries for raisins, etc. – without adversely affecting the finished product. However, avoid using fresh fruit as the juice will react badly with the dough.

Baking cookies is creative, enjoyable and simple – it is a great way to create something really tasty in a short space of time. Get in the kitchen and let the fun begin!

Classic
Favourites

Chocolate Chip Cookies

Makes 8

unsalted butter, melted,
    for greasing
175 g/6 oz plain flour, sifted
1 tsp baking powder
125 g/4½ oz margarine, melted
85 g/3 oz light muscovado sugar
55 g/2 oz caster sugar
½ tsp vanilla extract
1 egg
125 g/4½ oz plain chocolate chips

Preheat the oven to 190°C/375°F/Gas Mark 5. Lightly grease two baking sheets.

Place all of the ingredients in a large mixing bowl and beat until well combined.

Place tablespoons of the mixture on the prepared baking sheets, spaced well apart.

Bake in the preheated oven for 10–12 minutes, or until golden brown. Transfer to a wire rack and leave to cool.

variation
use milk chocolate chips
instead of plain
if preferred

Classic Oatmeal Cookies

Makes 30

175 g/6 oz butter or margarine,
   plus extra for greasing
275 g/9¾ oz demerara sugar
1 egg
4 tbsp water
1 tsp vanilla extract
375 g/13 oz rolled oats
140 g/5 oz plain flour
1 tsp salt
½ tsp bicarbonate of soda

Preheat the oven to 180°C/350°F/Gas Mark 4. Grease two large baking sheets.

Place the butter and sugar in a large bowl and beat together until light and fluffy. Beat in the egg, water and vanilla extract until the mixture is smooth. Mix the oats, flour, salt and bicarbonate of soda together in a separate bowl, then gradually stir the oat mixture into the creamed mixture until thoroughly combined.

Place tablespoonfuls of the mixture on the prepared baking sheets, spaced well apart.

Bake in the preheated oven for 15 minutes, or until golden brown. Transfer to a wire rack to cool completely.

variation
add sultanas to the
dough mix

White Chocolate Cookies

Makes 24

115 g/4 oz butter, softened,
  plus extra for greasing

115 g/4 oz soft light brown sugar

1 egg, lightly beaten

250 g/9 oz self-raising flour

pinch of salt

125 g/4½ oz white chocolate,
  chopped

50 g/1¾ oz Brazil nuts, chopped

Preheat the oven to 190°C/375°F/Gas Mark 5. Lightly grease several large baking sheets.

Place the butter and sugar in a large bowl and beat together until light and fluffy. Gradually add the egg, beating well after each addition.

Sift the flour and a pinch of salt into the creamed mixture and blend well. Stir in the chocolate chunks and chopped nuts.

Place heaped teaspoonfuls of the mixture on the prepared baking sheets, putting no more than six on each sheet because the cookies will spread during cooking.

Bake in the preheated oven for 10–12 minutes, or until just golden brown. Transfer the cookies to wire racks to cool completely.

great tip!
*chop chocolate
with a warm
knife to make easier*

Simple Cookies

Makes 25

175 g/6 oz plain flour,
   plus extra for dusting

¼ tsp ground nutmeg

115 g/4 oz unsalted butter,
   softened

50 g/1¾ oz caster sugar

Preheat the oven to 180°C/350°F/
Gas Mark 4.

Sift the flour and nutmeg into a large bowl.
Add the butter and rub it into the mixture
until it resembles breadcrumbs. Add the
sugar and knead together to form a
stiff dough.

Roll the dough out on a lightly floured work
surface to about 5 mm/¼ inch thick.

Using a 7-cm/2¾-inch round cookie cutter
dipped in flour, cut out 25 cookies. Re-roll
any trimmings. Place the cookies on two
large non-stick baking sheets.

Bake in the preheated oven for 8–10 minutes,
or until pale golden. Transfer to a wire rack
and leave to cool completely.

variation
add a sprinkle of
cinnamon to create spice

Oaty Raisin & Hazelnut Cookies

Makes about 30
55 g/2 oz raisins, chopped
125 ml/4 fl oz orange juice
225 g/8 oz butter, softened
140 g/5 oz caster sugar
1 egg yolk, lightly beaten
2 tsp vanilla extract
225 g/8 oz plain flour
pinch of salt
55 g/2 oz rolled oats
55 g/2 oz hazelnuts, chopped
whole hazelnuts, to decorate

Preheat the oven to 190°C/375°F/Gas Mark 5. Line two baking sheets with baking paper.

Put the raisins in a bowl, add the orange juice and leave to soak for 10 minutes.

Put the butter and sugar into a bowl and mix well with a wooden spoon, then beat in the egg yolk and vanilla extract.

Sift together the flour and a pinch of salt into the mixture and add the oats and chopped hazelnuts. Drain the raisins, add them to the mixture and stir until thoroughly combined.

Scoop up tablespoons of the mixture and place them in mounds on the prepared baking sheets, spaced well apart. Flatten slightly and place a whole hazelnut in the centre of each cookie.

Bake in the preheated oven for 12–15 minutes, until golden brown. Leave to cool on the baking sheets for 5–10 minutes, then, using a palette knife, carefully transfer the cookies to wire racks to cool completely.

Peanut Butter Cookies

Makes 12–15

175 g/6 oz plain flour

½ tsp baking powder

½ tsp salt

225 g/8 oz smooth peanut butter

115 g/4 oz butter, softened

1¼ tsp vanilla extract

115 g/4 oz brown sugar

100 g/3½ oz caster sugar

2 eggs

Sift together the flour, baking powder and salt into a bowl and set aside. Beat together the peanut butter, butter and vanilla extract until smooth in another bowl. Beat in the brown and caster sugar for 1 minute, then stir in the eggs one at a time. Stir in the flour mixture in two batches.

Wrap the dough in clingfilm and chill in the refrigerator for at least 2 hours. Meanwhile, preheat the oven to 180°C/350°F/Gas Mark 4. Line a baking sheet with baking paper or leave uncovered and ungreased.

Roll or scoop the dough into 4-cm/ 1½-inch balls and place them on the prepared baking sheet, spaced well apart. Use a fork to flatten each ball by making a criss-cross pattern. Bake in the preheated oven for 15 minutes, or until golden. Remove the biscuits from the oven and leave to cool on the baking sheet for 5 minutes. Using a palette knife, transfer to a wire rack and leave to cool.

Spiced Rum Cookies

Makes 18

175 g/6 oz unsalted butter, softened, plus extra for greasing

175 g/6 oz dark muscovado sugar

225 g/8 oz plain flour

pinch of salt

½ tsp bicarbonate of soda

1 tsp ground cinnamon

¼ tsp ground coriander

½ tsp ground nutmeg

¼ tsp ground cloves

2 tbsp dark rum

Preheat the oven to 180°C/350°F/ Gas Mark 4. Lightly grease two baking sheets.

Cream together the butter and sugar and whisk until light and fluffy.

Sift the flour, a pinch of salt, bicarbonate of soda, cinnamon, coriander, nutmeg and cloves into the creamed mixture. Stir the dark rum into the creamed mixture.

Place 18 spoonfuls of the dough on the prepared baking sheets, spaced well apart. Flatten each one slightly with the back of a spoon.

Bake in the preheated oven for 10–12 minutes until golden. Leave the biscuits to cool and crispen on wire racks before serving.

variation
add raisins to dough to create rum & raisin cookies

Cookies &
Cream Sandwiches

Makes about 15
125 g/4½ oz butter, softened
75 g/2¾ oz icing sugar
115 g/4 oz plain flour
40 g/1½ oz cocoa powder
½ tsp ground cinnamon

Filling
125 g/4½ oz plain chocolate,
    broken into pieces
50 ml/2 fl oz double cream

Preheat the oven to 160°C/325°F/Gas Mark 3. Line two large baking sheets with baking paper.

Place the butter and sugar in a large bowl and beat together until light and fluffy. Sift the flour, cocoa and cinnamon into the mixture and mix to form a dough.

Place the dough between two sheets of baking paper and roll out until the dough is 3 mm/⅛ inch thick. Cut out 6-cm/2½-inch rounds and place on the prepared baking sheets.

Bake in the preheated oven for 15 minutes, or until firm to the touch. Leave to cool for 2 minutes on the baking paper, then transfer the cookies to wire racks to cool completely.

Meanwhile, make the filling. Place the chocolate and cream in a saucepan and heat gently until the chocolate has melted. Stir until smooth. Leave to cool, then chill in the refrigerator for 2 hours, or until firm. Sandwich the biscuits together in pairs with a spoonful of the chocolate cream and serve.

Gingernuts

Makes 30

125 g/4½ oz butter,
    plus extra for greasing
350 g/12 oz self-raising flour
pinch of salt
200 g/7 oz caster sugar
1 tbsp ground ginger
1 tsp bicarbonate of soda
75 g/2¾ oz golden syrup
1 egg, beaten
1 tsp grated orange rind

Preheat the oven to 160°C/325°F/Gas Mark 3. Lightly grease several baking sheets.

Sift together the flour, a pinch of salt, sugar, ginger and bicarbonate of soda into a large mixing bowl.

Heat the butter and golden syrup together in a saucepan over a very low heat until the butter has melted. Remove the pan from the heat and leave to cool slightly, then pour the contents onto the dry ingredients.

Add the egg and orange rind and mix thoroughly to form a dough. Using your hands, carefully shape the dough into 30 even-sized balls.

Place the balls on the prepared baking sheets, spaced well apart, then flatten them slightly with your fingers.

Bake in the preheated oven for 15–20 minutes, then carefully transfer to a wire rack to cool.

Double Chocolate Cookies

Makes about 30
225 g/8 oz butter, softened
140 g/5 oz caster sugar
1 egg yolk, lightly beaten
2 tsp vanilla extract
250 g/9 oz plain flour
25 g/1 oz cocoa powder
pinch of salt
350 g/12 oz plain chocolate, chopped
55 g/2 oz dried sour cherries

Preheat the oven to 190°C/375°F/Gas Mark 5. Line two baking sheets with baking paper.

Put the butter and sugar into a bowl and mix well with a wooden spoon, then beat in the egg yolk and vanilla extract. Sift together the flour, cocoa and a pinch of salt into the mixture, add the chopped chocolate and sour cherries and stir until thoroughly combined.

Scoop up tablespoons of the mixture and shape into balls. Put them on the prepared baking sheets, spaced well apart, and flatten slightly.

Bake in the preheated oven for 12–15 minutes. Leave to cool on the baking sheets for 5–10 minutes, then, using a palette knife, carefully transfer to wire racks to cool completely.

variation
replace plain chocolate with milk chocolate if preferred

Cinnamon & Caramel Cookies

Makes about 25
225 g/8 oz butter, softened
140 g/5 oz caster sugar
1 egg yolk, lightly beaten
1 tsp vanilla extract
280 g/10 oz plain flour
1 tsp ground cinnamon
½ tsp mixed spice
pinch of salt
25–30 caramel sweets

Preheat the oven to 190°C/375°F/Gas Mark 5. Line two baking sheets with baking paper.

Put the butter and sugar into a bowl and mix well with a wooden spoon, then beat in the egg yolk and vanilla extract. Sift together the flour, cinnamon, mixed spice and a pinch of salt into the mixture and stir until thoroughly combined.

Scoop up tablespoons of the mixture, shape into balls and place on the prepared baking sheets, spaced well apart. Bake in the preheated oven for 8 minutes. Place a caramel sweet on top of each cookie, return to the oven and bake for a further 6–7 minutes.

Remove from the oven and leave to cool on the baking sheets for 5–10 minutes. Using a palette knife, carefully transfer the cookies to wire racks to cool completely.

variation
replace the caramel sweet
with chocolate buttons

Mini Florentines

Makes 20–30

75 g/2¾ oz butter

75 g/2¾ oz caster sugar

25 g/1 oz sultanas or raisins

25 g/1 oz glacé cherries, chopped

25 g/1 oz crystallized stem ginger, finely chopped

25 g/1 oz sunflower seeds

100 g/3½ oz flaked almonds

2 tbsp double cream

175 g/6 oz plain or milk chocolate, broken into pieces

Preheat the oven to 180°C/350°F/Gas Mark 4. Line two baking sheets. Place the butter in a small saucepan and melt over a low heat. Add the sugar, stir until dissolved, then bring to the boil. Remove from the heat and stir in the sultanas, glacé cherries, crystallized ginger, sunflower seeds and almonds. Mix well, then beat in the cream.

Place teaspoons of the mixture on the prepared baking sheets, spaced well apart. Bake in the preheated oven for 10–12 minutes, or until light golden in colour. Remove from the oven and, while still hot, use a circular biscuit cutter to pull in the edges to form circles. Leave to cool and crisp before removing from the baking sheets.

Put the chocolate in a heatproof bowl set over a saucepan of gently simmering water and stir until melted. Spread most of the chocolate onto a sheet of baking paper. When the chocolate is on the point of setting, place the biscuits flat-side down on the chocolate and let it harden completely. Cut around the florentines and remove from the baking paper. Spread the remaining chocolate on the coated side of the florentines, using a fork. Leave to set.

Sticky Ginger Cookies

Makes 20

225 g/8 oz butter, softened

140 g/5 oz golden caster sugar

1 egg yolk, lightly beaten

55 g/2 oz stem ginger, roughly
  chopped, plus 1 tbsp syrup from
  the jar

280 g/10 oz plain flour

pinch of salt

55 g/2 oz plain chocolate chips

Put the butter and sugar into a bowl and mix well with a wooden spoon, then beat in the egg yolk and ginger syrup. Sift together the flour and a pinch of salt into the mixture, add the stem ginger and chocolate chips and stir until thoroughly combined.

Shape the mixture into a log, wrap in clingfilm and chill in the refrigerator for 30–60 minutes.

Preheat the oven to 190°C/375°F/Gas Mark 5. Line two baking sheets with baking paper.

Unwrap the log and cut it into 5-mm/ ¼-inch slices with a sharp serrated knife. Put them on the prepared baking sheets, spaced well apart.

Bake in the preheated oven for 12–15 minutes, until golden brown. Leave to cool on the baking sheets for 5–10 minutes, then, using a palette knife, carefully transfer the cookies to wire racks to cool completely.

Almond Crunchies

Makes about 50
225 g/8 oz butter, softened
140 g/5 oz caster sugar
1 egg yolk, lightly beaten
½ tsp almond extract
225 g/8 oz plain flour
pinch of salt
225 g/8 oz blanched almonds,
  chopped

Put the butter and sugar into a bowl and mix well with a wooden spoon, then beat in the egg yolk and almond extract. Sift together the flour and a pinch of salt into the mixture, add the almonds and stir until thoroughly combined. Halve the dough, shape it into balls, wrap in clingfilm and chill in the refrigerator for 30–60 minutes.

Preheat the oven to 190°C/375°F/Gas Mark 5. Line two to three baking sheets with baking paper.

Shape the dough into about 50 small balls and flatten them slightly between the palms of your hands. Put on the prepared baking sheets, spaced well apart. Bake in the preheated oven for 15–20 minutes, until golden brown. Leave to cool on the baking sheets for 5–10 minutes, then, using a palette knife, carefully transfer to wire racks to cool completely.

variation
press marzipan into the middle of each cookie before cooking

Jam Rings

Makes about 15
225 g/8 oz butter, softened
140 g/5 oz caster sugar,
    plus extra for sprinkling
1 egg yolk, lightly beaten
2 tsp vanilla extract
280 g/10 oz plain flour
pinch of salt
1 egg white, lightly beaten

Jam filling
55 g/2 oz butter, softened
100 g/3½ oz icing sugar
5 tbsp strawberry or
    raspberry jam

Put the butter and caster sugar into a bowl and mix well, then beat in the egg yolk and vanilla extract. Sift together the flour and a pinch of salt into the mixture and stir. Halve the dough, shape into balls, wrap in clingfilm and chill in the refrigerator for 30–60 minutes.

Preheat the oven to 190°C/375°F/Gas Mark 5. Line two baking sheets with baking paper. Unwrap the dough and roll out between two sheets of baking paper. Stamp out cookies with a 7-cm/2¾-inch fluted round cutter and put half of them on a prepared baking sheet, spaced well apart. Using a 4-cm/1½-inch plain round cutter, stamp out the centres of the remaining cookies and remove. Put the cookie rings on the other baking sheet, spaced well apart.

Bake for 7 minutes, then brush the cookie rings with beaten egg white and sprinkle with caster sugar. Bake for a further 5–8 minutes, until light golden brown. Leave to cool on the baking sheets for 5–10 minutes, then carefully transfer to wire racks to cool completely. To make filling, beat the butter and icing sugar together in a bowl. Spread the buttercream over the whole cookies and top with jam. Place the cookie rings on top and press together.

Biscotti

Makes about 30
225 g/8 oz butter, softened
140 g/5 oz caster sugar
finely grated rind of 1 lemon
1 egg yolk, lightly beaten
2 tsp brandy
280 g/10 oz plain flour
pinch of salt
85 g/3 oz pistachio nuts
icing sugar, for dusting

Put the butter, caster sugar and lemon rind into a bowl and mix well with a wooden spoon, then beat in the egg yolk and brandy. Sift together the flour and a pinch of salt into the mixture and stir in the pistachio nuts until thoroughly combined.

Shape the mixture into a log, flatten slightly, wrap in clingfilm and chill in the refrigerator for 30–60 minutes.

Preheat the oven to 190°C/375°F/Gas Mark 5. Line two baking sheets with baking paper.

Unwrap the log and cut it slightly on the diagonal into 5-mm/$\frac{1}{4}$-inch slices with a sharp serrated knife. Put them on the prepared baking sheets, spaced well apart.

Bake in the preheated oven for 10 minutes, until golden brown. Leave to cool on the baking sheets for 5–10 minutes, then, using a palette knife, carefully transfer to wire racks to cool completely. Dust with icing sugar.

Mixed Fruit Cookies

Makes about 30

225 g/8 oz butter, softened

140 g/5 oz caster sugar

1 egg yolk, lightly beaten

280 g/10 oz plain flour

½ tsp mixed spice

pinch of salt

25 g/1 oz ready-to-eat dried
apple, chopped

25 g/1 oz ready-to-eat dried pear,
chopped

25 g/1 oz ready-to-eat prunes,
chopped

grated rind of 1 orange

Put the butter and sugar into a bowl and mix well with a wooden spoon, then beat in the egg yolk. Sift together the flour, mixed spice and a pinch of salt into the mixture. Add the apple, pear, prunes and orange rind and stir until thoroughly combined. Shape the dough into a log, wrap in clingfilm and chill in the refrigerator for 30–60 minutes.

Preheat the oven to 190°C/375°F/Gas Mark 5. Line two baking sheets with baking paper.

Unwrap the log and cut it into 5 mm/ ¼ inch thick slices with a sharp serrated knife. Put them on the prepared baking sheets, spaced well apart.

Bake in the preheated oven for 10–15 minutes, until golden brown. Leave to cool on the baking sheets for 5–10 minutes, then, using a palette knife, carefully transfer the cookies to wire racks to cool completely.

Butter Cookies

Makes 25

125 g/4½ oz unsalted butter, softened

125 g/4½ oz caster sugar

1 large egg yolk

100 g/3½ oz plain flour

1 tsp ground cinnamon

Preheat the oven to 200°C/400°F/Gas Mark 6. Line a large baking sheet with baking paper.

Place the butter and 25 g/1 oz of the sugar in a large bowl and beat together until light and fluffy. Add the egg yolk and stir together, then sift in the flour and mix to form a soft dough.

Mix the remaining sugar with the cinnamon. Take a teaspoon of dough and roll it in the sugar mixture. Place on the prepared baking sheet and use a fork to press down until the cookie is 1 cm/½ inch thick. Repeat until all the dough is used up.

Bake in the preheated oven for 10 minutes, or until golden brown. Transfer to a wire rack and leave to cool.

variation
add 100 g/3½ oz shredded coconut to dough and omit the cinnamon

Healthy Wholemeal Cookies

Makes 36

300 g/10½ oz plain wholemeal flour, plus extra for dusting

2 tbsp wheatgerm

¼ tsp bicarbonate of soda

½ tsp salt

50 g/1¾ oz caster sugar

125 g/4½ oz unsalted butter, cubed

1 large egg, lightly beaten

1 tsp vanilla extract

Preheat the oven to 160°C/325°F/Gas Mark 3.

Place the flour, wheatgerm, bicarbonate of soda, salt and sugar in a large bowl and stir together until combined. Add the butter and rub it in until the mixture resembles breadcrumbs.

Whisk the egg and vanilla extract in a separate bowl and add to the mixture, adding a little cold water if needed to bring the dough together. Roll the dough out on a floured board. Use a 7-cm/2¾-inch floured cookie cutter to cut out the biscuits and place them on non-stick baking sheets, re-rolling the dough when necessary.

Bake in the preheated oven for 20–25 minutes, or until dry but not brown. Transfer to a wire rack and leave to cool.

variation
add 2 tbsp of chopped currants to the dough

Chocolate Orange Cookies

Makes 30

90 g/3¼ oz butter, softened

60 g/2¼ oz caster sugar

1 egg

1 tbsp milk

280 g/10 oz plain flour,
    plus extra for dusting

2 tbsp cocoa powder

To decorate

175 g/6 oz icing sugar

3 tbsp orange juice

a little plain chocolate,
    broken into pieces

Preheat the oven to 180°C/350°F/Gas Mark 4. Line two large baking sheets with baking paper. Place the butter and caster sugar in a large bowl and beat together until light and fluffy. Beat in the egg and milk until thoroughly combined. Sift the flour and cocoa into the bowl and gradually mix together to form a soft dough.

Roll out the dough on a lightly floured work surface until about 5 mm/¼ inch thick. Cut out rounds with a 5-cm/2-inch fluted round cookie cutter and place them on the baking sheets. Bake in the preheated oven for 10–12 minutes, or until golden. Leave to cool on the baking sheet for a few minutes, then transfer the cookies to a wire rack to cool completely and become crisp.

To make the icing, sift the icing sugar in a bowl and stir in enough orange juice to form a thin icing that will coat the back of the spoon. Place a spoonful of icing in the centre of each cookie and leave to set.

Place the chocolate in a heatproof bowl, set the bowl over a saucepan of gently simmering water and heat until melted. Drizzle thin lines of melted chocolate over the biscuits and leave to set before serving.

Chocolate
Choice

Mega Chip Cookies

Makes 12

225 g/8 oz butter, softened

140 g/5 oz caster sugar

1 egg yolk, lightly beaten

2 tsp vanilla extract

225 g/8 oz plain flour

55 g/2 oz cocoa powder

pinch of salt

85 g/3 oz milk chocolate chips

85 g/3 oz white chocolate chips

115 g/4 oz plain chocolate,
   roughly chopped

Preheat the oven to 190°C/375°F/Gas Mark 5. Line three baking sheets with baking paper.

Put the butter and sugar into a bowl and mix well with a wooden spoon, then beat in the egg yolk and vanilla extract. Sift together the flour, cocoa powder and a pinch of salt into the mixture, add both kinds of chocolate chips and stir until thoroughly combined.

Make 12 balls of the mixture, put them on to the prepared baking sheets, spaced well apart, and flatten slightly. Press the pieces of plain chocolate into the cookies.

Bake in the preheated oven for 12–15 minutes. Leave to cool on the baking sheets for 5–10 minutes, then, using a palette knife, carefully transfer to wire racks to cool completely.

variation
replace a chocolate chip
with chopped caramels

Chocolate Chip & Cinnamon Cookies

Makes about 30

225 g/8 oz butter, softened

140 g/5 oz caster sugar

1 egg yolk, lightly beaten

2 tsp orange extract

280 g/10 oz plain flour

pinch of salt

100 g/3½ oz plain chocolate chips

Cinnamon coating

1½ tbsp caster sugar

1½ tbsp ground cinnamon

Preheat the oven to 190°C/375°F/Gas Mark 5. Line two baking sheets with baking paper.

Put the butter and sugar into a bowl and mix well with a wooden spoon, then beat in the egg yolk and orange extract. Sift together the flour and a pinch of salt into the mixture, add the chocolate chips and stir until thoroughly combined.

For the cinnamon coating, mix together the caster sugar and cinnamon in a shallow dish. Scoop out tablespoons of the cookie dough, roll them into balls, then roll them in the cinnamon mixture to coat. Put them on the prepared baking sheets, spaced well apart.

Bake in the preheated oven for 12–15 minutes. Leave to cool on the baking sheets for 5–10 minutes, then, using a palette knife, carefully transfer to wire racks to cool completely.

variation
use white chocolate chips
instead of plain

Midnight Cookies

Makes 25
125 g/4½ oz butter, softened
175 g/6 oz caster sugar
1 egg, lightly beaten
½ tsp vanilla extract
125 g/4½ oz plain flour
35 g/1¼ oz cocoa powder
½ tsp bicarbonate of soda

Preheat the oven to 180°C/350°F/Gas Mark 4. Line several large baking sheets with baking paper.

Place the butter and sugar in a large bowl and beat together until light and fluffy. Add the egg and vanilla extract and mix until smooth. Sift in the flour, cocoa and bicarbonate of soda and beat until well mixed.

With dampened hands, roll walnut-sized pieces of the dough into smooth balls. Place on the prepared baking sheets, spaced well apart.

Bake in the preheated oven for 10–12 minutes, or until set. Leave to cool on the baking sheets for 5 minutes, then transfer the cookies to wire racks to cool completely before serving.

variation
for a sugar coating, roll each cookie dough ball in sugar

Chocolate Mint Cookie Sandwiches

Makes about 15
225 g/8 oz butter, softened
140 g/5 oz caster sugar
1 egg yolk, lightly beaten
2 tsp vanilla extract
250 g/9 oz plain flour
25 g/1 oz cocoa powder
pinch of salt
55 g/2 oz glacé cherries, finely
    chopped
15 after-dinner mints

Chocolate coating
115 g/4 oz plain chocolate,
    broken into pieces
55 g/2 oz white chocolate,
    broken into pieces

Put the butter and sugar into a bowl and mix well with a wooden spoon, then beat in the egg yolk and vanilla extract. Sift together the flour, cocoa powder and a pinch of salt into the mixture, add the cherries and stir. Halve the dough, shape into balls, wrap in clingfilm and chill for 30–60 minutes.

Preheat the oven to 190°C/375°F/Gas Mark 5. Line two baking sheets with baking paper. Unwrap the dough and roll out between two sheets of baking paper. Stamp out cookies with a 6-cm/2½-inch plain square cutter and put them on the prepared baking sheets, spaced well apart. Bake for 10–15 minutes, until firm. Immediately place an after-dinner mint on top of half the cookies, then cover with the remaining cookies.

For the chocolate coating, melt the plain chocolate in a heatproof bowl set over a pan of gently simmering water. Remove from the heat and leave to cool. Put the cookies on a wire rack over a sheet of baking paper. Spoon the plain chocolate over them, then tap the rack to level the surface and leave to set. Melt the white chocolate in a heatproof bowl set over a pan of gently simmering water. Remove from the heat and leave to cool. Pipe over the cookies, then leave to set.

Chocolate & Orange Cookie Sandwiches

Makes about 15

225 g/8 oz butter, softened

140 g/5 oz caster sugar

2 tsp finely grated orange rind

1 egg yolk, lightly beaten

2 tsp vanilla extract

250 g/9 oz plain flour

25 g/1 oz cocoa powder

pinch of salt

100 g/3½ oz plain chocolate,
  finely chopped

Filling

125 ml/4 fl oz double cream

200 g/7 oz white chocolate,
  broken into pieces

1 tsp orange extract

Preheat the oven to 190°C/375°F/Gas Mark 5. Line two baking sheets with baking paper.

Put the butter, sugar and orange rind into a bowl and mix well with a wooden spoon, then beat in the egg yolk and vanilla extract. Sift together the flour, cocoa powder and a pinch of salt into the mixture, add the chopped chocolate and stir until thoroughly combined.

Scoop up tablespoons of the dough, roll into balls and place on the prepared baking sheets, spaced well apart. Gently flatten and smooth the tops with the back of a spoon.

Bake in the preheated oven for 10–15 minutes, until light golden brown. Leave to cool on the baking sheets for 5–10 minutes, then, using a palette knife, carefully transfer to wire racks to cool completely.

To make the filling, bring the cream to the boil in a small saucepan, then remove the pan from the heat. Stir in the chocolate until the mixture is smooth, then stir in the orange extract. When the mixture is completely cool, use to sandwich the cookies together in pairs.

Mocha Walnut Cookies

Makes about 16

115 g/4 oz butter, softened,
   plus extra for greasing

115 g/4 oz light muscovado sugar

85 g/3 oz caster sugar

1 tsp vanilla extract

1 tbsp instant coffee granules,
   dissolved in 1 tbsp hot water

1 egg

175 g/6 oz plain flour

½ tsp baking powder

¼ tsp bicarbonate of soda

55 g/2 oz milk chocolate chips

55 g/2 oz walnut halves,
   roughly chopped

Preheat the oven to 180°C/350°F/Gas Mark 4. Grease two large baking sheets.

Place the butter and sugars in a large bowl and beat together until light and fluffy. Place the vanilla extract, coffee and egg in a separate bowl and whisk together. Gradually add the coffee mixture to the butter and sugar, beating until fluffy. Sift the flour, baking powder and bicarbonate of soda into the mixture and fold in carefully. Fold in the chocolate chips and walnuts.

Spoon heaped teaspoons of the mixture on the prepared baking sheets, spaced well apart. Bake in the preheated oven for 10–15 minutes, or until crisp on the outside but soft inside. Leave to cool on the baking sheets for 2 minutes, then transfer to wire racks to cool completely.

variation
*add flaked almonds instead
of walnuts*

Chocolate Sprinkle Cookies

Makes about 30
225 g/8 oz butter, softened
140 g/5 oz caster sugar
1 egg yolk, lightly beaten
2 tsp vanilla extract
225 g/8 oz plain flour,
    plus extra for dusting
55 g/2 oz cocoa powder
pinch of salt

To decorate
200 g/7 oz white chocolate,
    broken into pieces
85 g/3 oz chocolate vermicelli

Put the butter and sugar into a bowl and mix well with a wooden spoon, then beat in the egg yolk and vanilla extract. Sift together the flour, cocoa powder and a pinch of salt into the mixture and stir until thoroughly combined. Halve the dough, roll each piece into a ball, wrap in clingfilm and chill in the refrigerator for 30–60 minutes to firm up.

Preheat the oven to 190°C/375°F/Gas Mark 5. Line two baking sheets with baking paper. Unwrap the dough and roll out between two pieces of baking paper to about 5 mm/¼ inch thick and stamp out 30 cookies with a 6–7-cm/2½–2¾-inch fluted round cutter. Put them on the prepared baking sheets, spaced well apart.

Bake in the preheated oven for 10–12 minutes. Leave to cool on the baking sheets for 5–10 minutes, then carefully transfer the cookies to wire racks to cool completely. Put the pieces of white chocolate into a heatproof bowl and melt over a pan of gently simmering water, then immediately remove from the heat. Spread the melted chocolate over the cookies, leave to cool slightly and then sprinkle with the chocolate vermicelli. Leave to cool and set.

Chocolate Fudge Squares

Makes about 30
225 g/8 oz butter, softened
140 g/5 oz golden caster sugar
1 egg yolk, lightly beaten
2 tsp vanilla extract
225 g/8 oz plain flour
55 g/2 oz cocoa powder
pinch of salt

Chocolate fudge topping
8 chocolate-coated fudge fingers,
    broken into pieces
4 tbsp double cream

Put the butter and sugar into a bowl and mix well with a wooden spoon, then beat in the egg yolk and vanilla extract. Sift together the flour, cocoa and a pinch of salt into the mixture and stir until thoroughly combined. Halve the dough, shape into balls, wrap in clingfilm and chill in the refrigerator for 30–60 minutes. Preheat the oven to 190°C/375°F/Gas Mark 5. Line two baking sheets with baking paper.

Unwrap the dough and roll out between two sheets of baking paper to about 3 mm/⅛ inch thick. Stamp out cookies with a 6-cm/2½-inch square cutter and put them on the prepared baking sheets, spaced well apart. Bake in the preheated oven for 10–15 minutes, until golden brown. Leave to cool on the baking sheets for 5–10 minutes, then, using a palette knife, carefully transfer the cookies to wire racks to cool completely.

For the chocolate fudge topping, put the fudge fingers into a heatproof bowl and melt over a pan of gently simmering water. Remove the bowl from the heat and gradually whisk in the cream. Leave to cool, then chill until spreadable. Spread the fudge topping over the cookies before serving.

Chocolate Spread & Hazelnut Drops

Makes about 30

225 g/8 oz butter, softened

140 g/5 oz caster sugar

1 egg yolk, lightly beaten

2 tsp vanilla extract

225 g/8 oz plain flour

55 g/2 oz cocoa powder

pinch of salt

55 g/2 oz ground hazelnuts

55 g/2 oz plain chocolate chips

4 tbsp chocolate and hazelnut
spread

Preheat the oven to 190°C/375°F/Gas Mark 5. Line two baking sheets with baking paper.

Put the butter and sugar into a bowl and mix well with a wooden spoon, then beat in the egg yolk and vanilla extract. Sift together the flour, cocoa and a pinch of salt into the mixture, add the ground hazelnuts and chocolate chips and stir until thoroughly combined.

Scoop out tablespoons of the mixture and shape into balls with your hands, then put them on the prepared baking sheets, spaced well apart. Use the dampened handle of a wooden spoon to make a hollow in the centre of each cookie.

Bake in the preheated oven for 12–15 minutes. Leave to cool on the baking sheets for 5–10 minutes, then, using a palette knife, carefully transfer the cookies to wire racks to cool completely. When they are cold, fill the hollows in the centre with the chocolate and hazelnut spread.

Chocolate Wholemeals

Makes 20
75 g/2¾ oz butter,
    plus extra for greasing
125 g/4½ oz demerara sugar
1 egg
1 tbsp wheatgerm
150 g/5½ oz wholewheat
    self-raising flour
70 g/2½ oz self-raising flour
125 g/4½ oz plain chocolate,
    broken into pieces

Preheat the oven to 180°C/350°F/Gas Mark 4. Lightly grease two large baking sheets.

Place the butter and sugar in a large bowl and beat together until light and fluffy. Add the egg and beat well. Stir in the wheatgerm and flours, then bring the mixture together with your hands. Roll rounded teaspoonfuls of the mixture into balls and place them on the prepared baking sheets, spaced well apart, then flatten slightly with the tines of a fork.

Bake in the preheated oven for 15–20 minutes, or until golden brown. Leave to cool for a few minutes, then transfer the cookies to a wire rack to cool completely.

Place the chocolate in a heatproof bowl, set the bowl over a saucepan of gently simmering water and heat until melted. Dip each biscuit in the chocolate to cover the flat side and a little way around the edges. Let the excess drip back into the bowl. Place the biscuits on a sheet of baking paper in a cool place and leave to set before serving.

Chocolate & Apricot Cookies

Makes about 30

225 g/8 oz butter, softened

140 g/5 oz caster sugar

1 egg yolk, lightly beaten

2 tsp amaretto liqueur

280 g/10 oz plain flour

pinch of salt

55 g/2 oz plain chocolate chips

55 g/2 oz ready-to-eat dried
   apricots, chopped

100 g/3½ oz blanched almonds,
   chopped

Place the butter and sugar in a large bowl and beat together until light and fluffy, then beat in the egg yolk and amaretto liqueur. Sift together the flour and a pinch of salt into the mixture, add the chocolate chips and apricots and stir until thoroughly combined.

Shape the mixture into a log. Spread out the almonds in a shallow dish and roll the log in them to coat. Wrap in clingfilm and chill in the refrigerator for 30–60 minutes.

Preheat the oven to 190°C/375°F/Gas Mark 5. Line two large baking sheets with baking paper. Unwrap the dough, cut into 5-mm/¼-inch slices with a sharp serrated knife and place them on the prepared baking sheets, spaced well apart.

Bake in the preheated oven for 12–15 minutes, or until golden brown. Leave to cool for 5–10 minutes, then transfer the cookies to wire racks to cool completely.

White Chocolate & Plum Cookies

Makes about 30
225 g/8 oz butter, softened
140 g/5 oz caster sugar
1 egg yolk, lightly beaten
2 tsp vanilla extract
225 g/8 oz plain flour
55 g/2 oz cocoa powder
pinch of salt
100 g/3½ oz white chocolate,
  chopped

To decorate
55 g/2 oz white chocolate,
  broken into pieces
15 ready-to-eat dried plums,
  halved

Place the butter and sugar in a large bowl and beat together until fluffy, then beat in the egg yolk and vanilla extract. Sift the flour, cocoa and salt into the mixture and stir. Halve the dough, shape into balls, wrap in clingfilm and chill for 30–60 minutes.

Preheat the oven to 190°C/ 375°F/Gas Mark 5. Line two large baking sheets with baking paper. Unwrap a ball of dough and roll out between two sheets of baking paper to about 3 mm/⅛ inch thick. Cut out 15 rounds with a plain 5-cm/2-inch cutter and place them on the prepared baking sheets, spaced well apart. Divide the chopped chocolate among the cookies.

Roll out the remaining dough between two sheets of baking paper and cut out rounds with a 6–7-cm/2½–2¾-inch cutter. Place them on top of the first cookies and press together to seal. Bake in the preheated oven for 10–15 minutes until firm. Leave to cool for 5–10 minutes, then transfer the cookies to wire racks to cool completely. To decorate, place the chocolate in a heatproof bowl, set the bowl over a saucepan of simmering water and heat until melted. Leave to cool. Dip the plums into the melted chocolate and stick in the middle of the cookies. Spoon the remaining chocolate over them and leave to set.

Chocolate Party Cookies

Makes 15

100 g/3½ oz butter

100 g/3½ oz soft light brown sugar

1 tbsp golden syrup

150 g/5½ oz self-raising flour

85 g/3 oz sugar-coated chocolates

Preheat the oven to 180°C/350°F/ Gas Mark 4. Line several large baking sheets with baking paper. Place the butter and sugar in a large bowl and whisk together until pale and creamy, then whisk the golden syrup into the mixture until smooth. Add 75 g/2¾ oz flour and whisk together until mixed. Stir in the sugar-coated chocolates and remaining flour then, with your hands, knead the mixture until smooth.

Roll small pieces of the dough between your hands into smooth balls to make 15 cookies in total and place them on the prepared baking sheets, spaced well apart. Bake in the preheated oven for 10–15 minutes, or until golden brown.

Leave on the baking sheets for 2–3 minutes, then transfer the cookies to a wire rack and leave to cool completely.

variation
use sugar-coated peanuts
instead

Choco Mint Stars

Makes about 30
225 g/8 oz butter, softened
140 g/5 oz caster sugar
1 egg yolk, lightly beaten
1 tsp peppermint extract
280 g/10 oz plain flour
pinch of salt
100 g/3½ oz desiccated coconut

To decorate
100 g/3½ oz white chocolate,
    broken into pieces
100 g/3½ oz milk chocolate,
    broken into pieces

Place the butter and sugar in a large bowl and beat together until light and fluffy, then beat in the egg yolk and peppermint extract. Sift together the flour and a pinch of salt into the mixture, add the coconut and stir until combined. Divide the mixture in half, shape into balls, wrap in clingfilm and chill in the refrigerator for 30–60 minutes.

Preheat the oven to 190°C/375°F/Gas Mark 5. Line two large baking sheets with baking paper. Unwrap the dough and roll out between two sheets of baking paper to about 3 mm/⅛ inch thick.

Cut out stars with a 6–7-cm/2½–2¾-inch cutter and place them on the baking sheets, spaced well apart. Bake in the preheated oven for 10–12 minutes, or until light golden. Leave to cool on the baking sheets for 5–10 minutes, then transfer the cookies to wire racks to cool completely.

Place the white chocolate and the milk chocolate in separate heatproof bowls, set the bowls over two saucepans of gently simmering water and heat until melted. Leave the cooled cookies on the racks and drizzle first with melted white chocolate and then with melted milk chocolate, using a teaspoon. Leave to set.

Giant Chocolate Chunk Cookies

Makes 12

115 g/4 oz butter, softened
125 g/4½ oz caster sugar
125 g/4½ oz soft light brown sugar
2 large eggs, lightly beaten
1 tsp vanilla extract
280 g/10 oz plain flour
1 tsp bicarbonate of soda
300 g/10½ oz chocolate chunks

Preheat the oven to 180°C/350°F/Gas Mark 4. Line several large baking sheets with baking paper.

Place the butter and sugars in a large bowl and whisk together until pale and creamy. Whisk the eggs and vanilla extract into the mixture until smooth. Sift in the flour and bicarbonate of soda and beat together until well mixed. Stir in the chocolate chunks.

Drop 12 large spoonfuls of the mixture on the prepared baking sheets, spaced well apart.

Bake in the preheated oven for 15–20 minutes, or until set and golden brown. Leave to cool on the baking sheets for 2–3 minutes, then transfer the cookies to a wire rack and leave to cool completely.

variation
use milk, white or plain chocolate chunks for variety

Chocolate & Coffee Wholemeal Cookies

Makes 24

175 g/6 oz butter,
   plus extra for greasing
200 g/7 oz soft light brown sugar
1 egg
70 g/2½ oz plain flour,
   plus extra for dusting (optional)
1 tsp bicarbonate of soda
pinch of salt
70 g/2½ oz wholemeal flour
1 tbsp bran
225 g/8 oz plain chocolate chips
185 g/6½ oz rolled oats
1 tbsp strong coffee
100 g/3½ oz hazelnuts,
   toasted and roughly chopped

Preheat the oven to 190°C/375°F/Gas Mark 5. Grease two large baking sheets. Place the butter and sugar in a large bowl and beat together until light and fluffy. Add the egg and beat well. Sift together the plain flour, bicarbonate of soda and a pinch of salt into another bowl, then add in the wholemeal flour and bran. Mix in the egg mixture, then stir in the chocolate chips, oats, coffee and hazelnuts and mix well.

Place 24 rounded tablespoons of the mixture on the baking sheets, spaced well apart. Alternatively, with lightly floured hands, break off pieces of the mixture and roll into balls (about 25 g/1 oz each), place on the prepared baking sheets and flatten.

Bake in the preheated oven for 16–18 minutes, or until golden brown. Leave to cool for 5 minutes, then transfer to a wire rack to cool completely.

great tip!
sandwich these cookies together with chocolate ice-cream

Chocolate & Banana Cookies

Makes about 20
125 g/4½ oz butter
125 g/4½ oz caster sugar
1 large egg, lightly beaten
1 ripe banana
175 g/6 oz self-raising flour
1 tsp mixed spice
2 tbsp milk
100 g/3½ oz chocolate,
   cut into chunks
55 g/2 oz raisins

Preheat the oven to 190°C/375°F/Gas Mark 5. Line two large baking sheets with baking paper.

Place the butter and sugar in a large bowl and beat together until light and fluffy. Gradually add the egg, beating well after each addition. Mash the banana and add it to the mixture, beating well until smooth.

Sift together the flour and mixed spice into the mixture and fold in with a spatula. Add the milk to give a soft consistency, then fold in the chocolate and raisins. Drop dessertspoons of the mixture on the prepared baking sheets, spaced well apart. Bake in the centre of the preheated oven for 15–20 minutes, or until lightly golden. Leave to cool slightly, then transfer to a wire rack to cool completely.

variation
add toffee to the dough
mix to create banoffee cookies

Chocolate & Almond Biscotti

Makes 24

butter, for greasing

150 g/5½ oz blanched almonds

150 g/5½ oz plain chocolate,
  broken into pieces

250 g/9 oz plain flour,
  plus extra for dusting

1 tsp baking powder

150 g/5½ oz caster sugar

2 large eggs, lightly beaten

1 tsp vanilla extract

Preheat the oven to 160°C/325°F/Gas Mark 3. Grease a large baking sheet. Spread the almonds on another baking sheet and bake in the preheated oven for 5–10 minutes, or until toasted. Leave to cool.

Place the chocolate in a heatproof bowl, set the bowl over a saucepan of simmering water and heat until melted. Remove from the heat and stir until smooth, then leave to cool. Sift the flour and baking powder into a large bowl. Add the sugar, cooled almonds, chocolate, eggs and vanilla extract and mix together to form a soft dough. Turn the dough onto a lightly floured work surface and, with floured hands, knead for 2–3 minutes, or until smooth. Divide the dough in half and shape each portion into a log shape measuring about 5 cm/2 inches in diameter. Place the logs on the baking sheet and flatten until each is 2.5 cm/1 inch thick.

Bake in the preheated oven for 20–30 minutes, or until firm to the touch. Leave to cool for 15 minutes. Reduce the oven temperature to 150°C/300°F/Gas Mark 2. Using a serrated knife, cut the baked dough into 1 cm/½ inch thick slices and place on ungreased baking sheets. Bake in the oven for 10 minutes. Turn and bake for a further 10–15 minutes until crisp. Transfer to a wire rack to cool.

Orange & Chocolate Fingers

Makes about 35

225 g/8 oz butter, softened

140 g/5 oz caster sugar

grated rind of 1 orange

1 egg yolk, lightly beaten

2 tsp orange juice

280 g/10 oz plain flour

1 tsp ground ginger

pinch of salt

115 g/4 oz plain chocolate,
  broken into pieces

Put the butter, sugar and orange rind into a bowl and mix well with a wooden spoon, then beat in the egg yolk and orange juice. Sift together the flour, ginger and a pinch of salt into the mixture and stir until thoroughly combined. Shape the dough into a ball, wrap in clingfilm and chill in the refrigerator for 30–60 minutes.

Preheat the oven to 190°C/375°F/Gas Mark 5. Line two baking sheets with baking paper. Unwrap the dough and roll out between two sheets of baking paper to a rectangle. Using a sharp knife, cut it into 10 x 2-cm/4 x ¾-inch strips and put them on the prepared baking sheets, spaced well apart. Bake in the preheated oven for 10–12 minutes, until light golden brown. Leave to cool on the baking sheets for 5–10 minutes, then, using a palette knife, carefully transfer to wire racks to cool completely.

Put the pieces of chocolate into a heatproof bowl and melt over a pan of gently simmering water, then remove from the heat and leave to cool. When the chocolate is cool but not set, dip the cookies diagonally into it to half coat, then put on the wire racks and leave to set. You may find it easier to do this using tongs.

Chocolate Buttons

Makes about 30
2 sachets instant chocolate
  or fudge chocolate drink
1 tbsp hot water
225 g/8 oz butter, softened
140 g/5 oz caster sugar,
  plus extra for sprinkling
1 egg yolk, lightly beaten
280 g/10 oz plain flour
pinch of salt

Empty the chocolate drink sachets into a bowl and stir in the hot water to make a paste. Put the butter and sugar into a bowl and mix well with a wooden spoon, then beat in the egg yolk and chocolate paste. Sift together the flour and a pinch of salt into the mixture and stir until thoroughly combined. Halve the dough, shape into rounds, wrap in clingfilm and chill in the refrigerator for 30–60 minutes.

Preheat the oven to 190°C/375°F/Gas Mark 5. Line two baking sheets with baking paper.

Unwrap the dough and roll out between two sheets of baking paper to 3 mm/⅛ inch thick. Stamp out rounds with a plain 5-cm/2-inch cutter. Using a 3-cm/1¼-inch cap from a soft drink or mineral water bottle, make an indentation in the centre of each button. Using a wooden toothpick, make four holes in the centre of each button, then put them on the prepared baking sheets, spaced well apart. Sprinkle with caster sugar.

Bake in the preheated oven for 10–15 minutes, until firm. Leave to cool on the baking sheets for 5–10 minutes, then, using a palette knife, transfer to wire racks to cool completely.

Fabulous
Fruit & Nut

Coconut &
Cranberry Cookies

Makes about 30
225 g/8 oz butter, softened
140 g/5 oz caster sugar
1 egg yolk, lightly beaten
2 tsp vanilla extract
280 g/10 oz plain flour
pinch of salt
40 g/1½ oz desiccated coconut
60 g/2¼ oz dried cranberries

Preheat the oven to 190°C/375°F/Gas Mark 5. Line two baking sheets with baking paper.

Put the butter and sugar into a bowl and mix well with a wooden spoon, then beat in the egg yolk and vanilla extract. Sift together the flour and a pinch of salt into the mixture, add the coconut and cranberries and stir until thoroughly combined.

Scoop up tablespoons of the dough and place in mounds on the prepared baking sheets, spaced well apart.

Bake in the preheated oven for 12–15 minutes, until golden brown. Leave to cool on the baking sheets for 5–10 minutes, then, using a palette knife, carefully transfer to wire racks to cool completely.

variation
replace the cranberries
with dried blueberries

Walnut & Coffee Cookies

Makes about 30
2 sachets instant latte
1 tbsp hot water
225 g/8 oz butter, softened
140 g/5 oz caster sugar
1 egg yolk, lightly beaten
280 g/10 oz plain flour
pinch of salt
100 g/3½ oz walnuts,
    finely chopped
coffee sugar crystals,
    for sprinkling

Put the instant latte into a bowl and stir in the hot water to make a paste. Put the butter and sugar into a bowl and mix well with a wooden spoon, then beat in the egg yolk and coffee paste. Sift together the flour and a pinch of salt into the mixture, add the walnuts and stir until thoroughly combined. Halve the dough, shape into balls, wrap in clingfilm and chill in the refrigerator for 30–60 minutes.

Preheat the oven to 190°C/375°F/Gas Mark 5. Line two baking sheets with baking paper.

Unwrap the dough and roll out between two sheets of baking paper to about 3 mm/⅛ inch thick. Stamp out rounds with a 6-cm/2½ -inch cutter and put them on the prepared baking sheets, spaced well apart.

Lightly brush the cookies with water, sprinkle with the coffee sugar crystals and bake in the preheated oven for 10–12 minutes. Leave to cool on the baking sheets for 5–10 minutes, then, using a palette knife, carefully transfer the cookies to wire racks to cool completely.

Banana & Raisin Cookies

Makes about 30
25 g/1 oz raisins
125 ml/4 fl oz orange juice or rum
225 g/8 oz butter, softened
140 g/5 oz caster sugar
1 egg yolk, lightly beaten
280 g/10 oz plain flour
pinch of salt
85 g/3 oz dried bananas,
    finely chopped

Put the raisins into a bowl, pour in the orange juice or rum and leave to soak for 30 minutes. Drain the raisins, reserving any remaining orange juice or rum.

Preheat the oven to 190°C/375°F/Gas Mark 5. Line two baking sheets with baking paper.

Put the butter and sugar into a bowl and mix well with a wooden spoon, then beat in the egg yolk and 2 teaspoons of the reserved orange juice or rum. Sift together the flour and a pinch of salt into the mixture, add the raisins and dried bananas and stir until thoroughly combined.

Put tablespoons of the mixture into heaps on the prepared baking sheets, spaced well apart, then flatten them gently. Bake in the preheated oven for 12–15 minutes, until golden. Leave to cool on the baking sheets for 5–10 minutes, then, using a palette knife, carefully transfer to wire racks to cool completely.

Almond Cookies with a Cherry on Top

Makes 25

200 g/7 oz butter, cut into cubes, plus extra for greasing

90 g/3¼ oz caster sugar

½ tsp almond extract

280 g/10 oz self-raising flour

25 g/1 oz ground almonds

25 glacé cherries (total weight about 125 g/4½ oz)

Preheat the oven to 180°C/350°F/Gas Mark 4. Grease several large baking sheets.

Place the butter in a large saucepan and heat gently until melted. Remove from the heat. Add the sugar and almond extract to the pan and stir together. Add the flour and ground almonds and mix to form a smooth dough.

Roll small pieces of the dough between your hands into smooth balls to make 25 in total. Place on the prepared baking sheets, spaced well apart, and flatten slightly with your hands, then press a cherry gently into the centre of each cookie. Bake in the preheated oven for 10–15 minutes, or until golden brown.

Leave to cool for 2–3 minutes on the baking sheets, then transfer the cookies to a wire rack to cool completely.

variation
replace the cherries with dried apricots

Apple Spice Cookies

Makes about 15

225 g/8 oz butter, softened

140 g/5 oz caster sugar

1 egg yolk, lightly beaten

2 tsp apple juice

280 g/10 oz plain flour

½ tsp ground cinnamon

½ tsp mixed spice

pinch of salt

100 g/3½ oz ready-to-eat dried apple, finely chopped

Filling

1 tbsp caster sugar

1 tbsp custard powder

125 ml/4 fl oz milk

5 tbsp apple sauce

Place the butter and sugar in a large bowl and beat together until light and fluffy, then beat in the egg yolk and apple juice. Sift together the flour, cinnamon, mixed spice and a pinch of salt into the mixture. Add the apple and stir until combined. Halve the dough, shape into balls, wrap in clingfilm and chill for 30–60 minutes.

Preheat the oven to 190°C/375°F/Gas Mark 5. Line two large baking sheets with baking paper. Unwrap the dough and roll out between two sheets of baking paper. Cut out cookies with a 5-cm/2-inch square cutter and place them on the prepared baking sheets, spaced well apart. Bake in the preheated oven for 10–15 minutes or until light golden brown. Leave to cool for 5–10 minutes, then transfer to wire racks to cool completely.

To make the apple filling, mix the sugar, custard powder and milk together in a saucepan. Bring to the boil, stirring constantly, and cook until thickened. Remove the pan from the heat and stir in the apple sauce. Cover the surface with clingfilm and leave to cool.

Spread the filling over half the cookies and top with the remainder.

Pecan &
Maple Cookies

Makes 18

115 g/4 oz butter, softened,
   plus extra for greasing

85 g/3 oz pecan nuts

2 tbsp maple syrup

85 g/3 oz light muscovado sugar

1 large egg yolk, lightly beaten

115 g/4 oz self-raising flour

Preheat the oven to 190°C/375°F/Gas Mark 5. Lightly grease two baking sheets. Reserve 18 pecan halves and roughly chop the rest.

Place the butter, maple syrup and sugar in a bowl and beat together with a wooden spoon until light and fluffy. Beat in the egg yolk. Sift over the flour and add the chopped pecan nuts. Mix to a stiff dough.

Place 18 spoonfuls of the mixture on the prepared baking sheets, spaced well apart. Top each with a reserved pecan nut, pressing down gently.

Bake in the preheated oven for 10–12 minutes, until light golden brown. Leave the cookies on the baking sheets for 10 minutes, then transfer to a wire rack and leave to cool completely.

variation
replace the maple syrup
with honey and the pecans
with almonds

Blueberry & Cranberry Cinnamon Cookies

Makes about 30
225 g/8 oz butter, softened
140 g/5 oz caster sugar
1 egg yolk, lightly beaten
2 tsp vanilla extract
280 g/10 oz plain flour
1 tsp ground cinnamon
pinch of salt
55 g/2 oz dried blueberries
55 g/2 oz dried cranberries
55 g/2 oz pine kernels, chopped

Preheat the oven to 190°C/375°F/Gas Mark 5. Line two baking sheets with baking paper.

Put the butter and sugar into a bowl and mix well with a wooden spoon, then beat in the egg yolk and vanilla extract. Sift together the flour, cinnamon and a pinch of salt into the mixture, add the blueberries and cranberries and stir until thoroughly combined.

Spread out the pine kernels in a shallow dish. Scoop up tablespoons of the mixture and roll them into balls. Roll the balls in the pine kernels to coat, then place on the prepared baking sheets, spaced well apart, and flatten slightly.

Bake in the preheated oven for 10–15 minutes. Leave to cool on the baking sheets for 5–10 minutes, then, using a palette knife, carefully transfer the cookies to wire racks to cool completely.

Golden Hazelnut Cookies

Makes about 30
225 g/8 oz butter, softened
140 g/5 oz golden caster sugar
1 egg yolk, lightly beaten
225 g/8 oz plain flour
pinch of salt
55 g/2 oz ground hazelnuts

To decorate
225 g/8 oz plain chocolate,
 broken into pieces
about 30 hazelnuts

Put the butter and sugar into a bowl and mix well with a wooden spoon, then beat in the egg yolk. Sift together the flour and a pinch of salt into the mixture, add the ground hazelnuts and stir until thoroughly combined. Halve the dough, form into balls, wrap in clingfilm and chill in the refrigerator for 30–60 minutes.

Preheat the oven to 190°C/375°F/Gas Mark 5. Line two baking sheets with baking paper. Unwrap the dough and roll out between two sheets of baking paper. Stamp out rounds with a 6-cm/2½-inch plain cutter and put them on the prepared baking sheets, spaced well apart.

Bake in the preheated oven for 10–12 minutes, until golden brown. Leave to cool for 5-10 minutes, then carefully transfer the cookies to wire racks to cool. When the cookies are cool, place the wire racks over a sheet of baking paper. Put the chocolate into a heatproof bowl and melt over a pan of gently simmering water. Remove the bowl from the heat and leave to cool, then spoon the chocolate over the cookies. Gently tap the wire racks to level the surface and leave to set. Add a hazelnut to the centre of each cookie.

Lemon & Lime Cookies

Makes about 30

225 g/8 oz butter, softened

140 g/5 oz caster sugar

1 egg yolk, lightly beaten

2 tsp lime juice

280 g/10 oz plain flour

pinch of salt

finely grated rind of 1 lemon

To decorate

140 g/5 oz plain chocolate,
   broken into pieces

30 thinly pared strips of lime rind

Icing

1 tbsp lightly beaten egg white

1 tbsp lime juice

115 g/4 oz icing sugar

For the decoration, put the chocolate in a heatproof bowl and melt over a pan of gently simmering water. Remove from the heat and leave to cool slightly. Line a tray with baking paper. Dip the strips of lime rind into the melted chocolate until well coated, then put on tray to set.

Put the butter and caster sugar into a bowl and mix well with a wooden spoon, then beat in the egg yolk and lime juice. Sift together the flour and a pinch of salt into the mixture, add the lemon rind and stir. Halve the dough, shape into balls, wrap in clingfilm and chill in the refrigerator for 30–60 minutes.

Preheat the oven to 190°C/375°F/Gas Mark 5. Line two baking sheets with baking paper. Unwrap the dough and roll out between two sheets of baking paper to 3 mm/⅛ inch thick. Stamp out rounds with a 6-cm/2½-inch plain cutter and put on baking sheets. Bake in the preheated oven for 10–15 minutes, until golden brown. Leave to cool for 5–10 minutes, then transfer to wire racks to cool.

For the icing, mix together the egg white and lime juice. Gradually beat in the icing sugar until smooth. Ice the cookies and top with the chocolate-coated lime rind.

Orange & Lemon Cookies

Makes about 30
225 g/8 oz butter, softened
140 g/5 oz caster sugar
1 egg yolk, lightly beaten
280 g/10 oz plain flour
pinch of salt
finely grated rind of 1 orange
finely grated rind of 1 lemon

To decorate
1 tbsp lightly beaten egg white
1 tbsp lemon juice
115 g/4 oz icing sugar
few drops yellow food colouring
few drops orange food colouring
about 15 lemon jelly slices
about 15 orange jelly slices

Put the butter and caster sugar into a bowl and mix well with a wooden spoon, then beat in the egg yolk. Sift together the flour and a pinch of salt into the mixture and stir until thoroughly combined. Halve the dough and gently knead the orange rind into one half and the lemon rind into the other. Shape into balls, wrap in clingfilm and chill in the refrigerator for 30–60 minutes.

Preheat the oven to 190°C/375°F/Gas Mark 5. Line two baking sheets with baking paper. Unwrap the orange-flavoured dough and roll out between two sheets of baking paper. Stamp out rounds with a 6-cm/ 2½-inch cutter and put them on a prepared baking sheet, spaced well apart. Repeat with the lemon-flavoured dough but stamp out crescents.

Bake in the preheated oven for 10–15 minutes, until golden brown. Leave to cool for 5–10 minutes, then transfer to wire racks to cool. To decorate, mix together the egg white and lemon juice. Gradually beat in the icing sugar with a wooden spoon until smooth. Spoon half the icing into another bowl. Stir yellow food colouring into one bowl and orange into the other. Leave the cookies on the racks. Spread the icing over the cookies and decorate with the jelly slices. Leave to set.

Peanut Butter & Grape Jelly Cookies

Makes about 25
225 g/8 oz butter, softened
140 g/5 oz caster sugar
1 egg yolk, lightly beaten
2 tsp vanilla extract
100 g/3½ oz crunchy
   peanut butter
280 g/10 oz plain flour
pinch of salt
4 tbsp grape jelly

Preheat the oven to 190°C/375°F/Gas Mark 5. Line two baking sheets with baking paper.

Put the butter and sugar into a bowl and mix well with a wooden spoon, then beat in the egg yolk, vanilla extract and peanut butter. Sift together the flour and a pinch of salt into the mixture and stir until thoroughly combined.

Scoop out tablespoons of the mixture and shape into balls with your hands, then put them on the prepared baking sheets, spaced well apart. Use the dampened handle of a wooden spoon to make a hollow in the centre of each cookie and fill the hollows with grape jelly.

Bake in the preheated oven for 12–15 minutes, until golden brown. Leave to cool on the baking sheets for 5–10 minutes, then, using a palette knife, carefully transfer the cookies to wire racks to cool completely.

Iced Cherry Rings

Makes 15–18

115 g/4 oz unsalted butter,
   plus extra for greasing
85 g/3 oz golden caster sugar
1 egg yolk
finely grated rind of ½ lemon
200 g/7 oz plain flour,
   plus extra for dusting
55 g/2 oz glacé cherries, finely
   chopped

Icing
85 g/3 oz icing sugar, sifted
1½ tbsp lemon juice

Preheat the oven to 200°C/400°F/Gas Mark 6. Lightly grease two baking sheets.

Cream together the butter and caster sugar until pale and fluffy. Beat in the egg yolk and lemon rind. Sift in the flour, stir, then add the glacé cherries, mixing with your hands to a soft dough.

Roll out the dough on a lightly floured surface to about 5 mm/¼ inch thick. Stamp out 8-cm/3¼-inch rounds with a biscuit cutter. Stamp out the centre of each round with a 2.5-cm/1-inch cutter and place the rings on the prepared baking sheets. Re-roll any trimmings and cut more biscuits.

Bake in the preheated oven for 12–15 minutes, until firm and golden brown. Allow to cool on the baking sheets for 2 minutes, then transfer to a wire rack to cool completely.

For the icing, mix the icing sugar to a smooth paste with the lemon juice. Drizzle over the biscuits and leave to set.

Banana & Caramel Cookies

Makes about 30

225 g/8 oz butter, softened

140 g/5 oz caster sugar

1 egg yolk, lightly beaten

25 g/1 oz stem ginger, finely
    chopped, plus 2 tsp syrup
    from the jar

280 g/10 oz plain flour

pinch of salt

85 g/3 oz dried bananas,
    finely chopped

15 chocolate caramel sweets

Put the butter and sugar into a bowl and mix well with a wooden spoon, then beat in the egg yolk, ginger and ginger syrup. Sift together the flour and a pinch of salt into the mixture, add the bananas and stir until thoroughly combined. Halve the dough, shape into balls, wrap in clingfilm and chill in the refrigerator for 30–60 minutes.

Preheat the oven to 190°C/375°F/Gas Mark 5. Line two baking sheets with baking paper.

Unwrap the dough and roll out between two sheets of baking paper. Stamp out cookies with a 6-cm/2½-inch fluted round cutter and put half of them on the prepared baking sheets, spaced well apart. Place a chocolate caramel in the centre of each cookie, then top with the remaining cookies and pinch the edges of the rounds together.

Bake in the preheated oven for 10–15 minutes, until light golden brown. Leave to cool on the baking sheets for 5–10 minutes, then, using a palette knife, carefully transfer to wire racks to cool completely.

Chewy Candied Fruit Cookies

Makes about 30
225 g/8 oz butter, softened
140 g/5 oz caster sugar
1 egg yolk, lightly beaten
2 tsp vanilla extract
280 g/10 oz plain flour
pinch of salt

Candied topping
4 tbsp maple syrup
55 g/2 oz butter
55 g/2 oz caster sugar
115 g/4 oz ready-to-eat dried
    peaches, chopped
55 g/2 oz glacé cherries, chopped
55 g/2 oz chopped mixed peel
85 g/3 oz macadamia nuts,
    chopped
25 g/1 oz plain flour

Put the butter and sugar into a bowl and mix well with a wooden spoon, then beat in the egg yolk and vanilla extract. Sift together the flour and a pinch of salt into the mixture and stir until thoroughly combined. Halve the dough, shape into balls, wrap in clingfilm and chill for 30–60 minutes.

Preheat the oven to 190°C/375°F/Gas Mark 5. Line two baking sheets with baking paper. Unwrap the dough and roll out between two sheets of baking paper. Stamp out rounds with a 6-cm/2½-inch plain round cutter and put them on the prepared baking sheets, spaced well apart.

For the candied topping, put the syrup, butter and sugar into a saucepan and melt over a low heat, stirring occasionally. Meanwhile, put the fruit, mixed peel, nuts and flour into a bowl and mix well. When the syrup mixture is thoroughly combined, stir it into the fruit mixture. Divide the candied topping among the cookies, gently spreading it out to the edges.

Bake in the preheated oven for 10–15 minutes, until firm. Leave to cool on the baking sheets for 5–10 minutes, then, using a palette knife, carefully transfer the cookies to wire racks to cool completely.

Walnut & Fig Pinwheels

Makes about 30
225 g/8 oz butter, softened
200 g/7 oz caster sugar
1 egg yolk, lightly beaten
225 g/8 oz plain flour
pinch of salt
55 g/2 oz ground walnuts
280 g/10 oz dried figs, finely
    chopped
5 tbsp freshly brewed mint tea
2 tsp finely chopped fresh mint

Put the butter and 140 g/5 oz of the sugar into a bowl and mix well with a wooden spoon, then beat in the egg yolk. Sift together the flour and a pinch of salt into the mixture, add the ground walnuts and stir. Shape the dough into a ball, wrap in clingfilm and chill for 30–60 minutes.

Meanwhile, put the remaining sugar into a saucepan and stir in 125 ml/4 fl oz water, then add the figs, mint tea and chopped mint. Bring to the boil, stirring constantly, until the sugar has dissolved, then simmer gently for 5 minutes. Remove pan from heat and leave to cool.

Unwrap the dough and roll out between two sheets of baking paper into a 30-cm/ 12-inch square. Spread the fig filling evenly over the dough, then roll up like a Swiss roll. Wrap in clingfilm and chill in the refrigerator for 30 minutes. Preheat the oven to 190°C/375°F/Gas Mark 5. Line two baking sheets with baking paper. Unwrap the roll and cut into thin slices with a sharp serrated knife. Put the slices on the prepared baking sheets, spaced well apart. Bake in the preheated oven for 10–15 minutes, until golden brown. Leave to cool on the baking sheets for 5–10 minutes, then, using a palette knife, transfer to wire racks to cool completely.

Crunchy Nut & Honey Cookie Sandwiches

Makes about 30
300 g/10½ oz butter, softened
140 g/5 oz caster sugar
1 egg yolk, lightly beaten
2 tsp vanilla extract
280 g/10 oz plain flour
pinch of salt
40 g/1½ oz macadamia nuts,
   cashew nuts or pine kernels,
   chopped
85 g/3 oz icing sugar
85 g/3 oz clover or other
   set honey

Preheat the oven to 190°C/375°F/Gas Mark 5. Line two baking sheets with baking paper.

Put 225 g/8 oz of the butter and the caster sugar into a bowl and mix well with a wooden spoon, then beat in the egg yolk and vanilla extract. Sift together the flour and a pinch of salt into the mixture and stir until thoroughly combined.

Scoop up tablespoons of the dough and roll into balls. Put half of them on a prepared baking sheet, spaced well apart, and flatten gently. Spread out the nuts in a shallow dish and dip one side of the remaining dough balls into them, then place on the other baking sheet, nut side uppermost, and flatten gently.

Bake in the preheated oven for 10–15 minutes, until light golden brown. Leave to cool on the baking sheets for 5–10 minutes, then, using a palette knife, carefully transfer to wire racks to cool completely.

Beat the remaining butter with the icing sugar and honey until creamy and thoroughly mixed. Spread the honey mixture over the plain cookies and top with the nut-coated cookies.

Mango, Coconut & Ginger Cookies

Makes about 30

225 g/8 oz butter, softened

140 g/5 oz caster sugar

1 egg yolk, lightly beaten

55 g/2 oz stem ginger,
   chopped, plus 2 tsp syrup
   from the jar

280 g/10 oz plain flour

pinch of salt

55 g/2 oz ready-to-eat dried
   mango, chopped

100 g/3½ oz desiccated coconut

Place the butter and sugar in a large bowl and beat together until light and fluffy, then beat in the egg yolk and ginger syrup. Sift together the flour and a pinch of salt into the mixture, add the stem ginger and mango and stir until combined.

Spread out the coconut in a shallow dish. Shape the dough into a log and roll it in the coconut to coat. Wrap in clingfilm and chill in the refrigerator for 30–60 minutes.

Preheat the oven to 190°C/375°F/Gas Mark 5. Line two large baking sheets with baking paper. Unwrap the log and cut it into 5-mm/¼-inch slices with a sharp serrated knife and place them on the prepared baking sheets, spaced well apart.

Bake in the preheated oven for 12–15 minutes, or until light golden brown. Leave to cool on the baking sheets for 5–10 minutes, then transfer the cookies to wire racks to cool completely.

Crunchy Muesli Cookies

Makes 24

115 g/4 oz unsalted butter,
   softened, plus extra for greasing
85 g/3 oz demerara sugar
1 tbsp clear honey
115 g/4 oz self-raising flour
pinch of salt
60 g/2¼ oz ready-to-eat dried
   apricots, chopped
50 g/1¾ oz dried figs, chopped
115 g/4 oz porridge oats
1 tsp milk (optional)
40 g/1½ oz sultanas or cranberries
40 g/1½ oz walnut halves,
   chopped

Preheat the oven to 160°C/325°F/Gas Mark 3. Grease two large baking sheets.

Place the butter, sugar and honey in a saucepan and heat over a low heat until melted. Mix to combine. Sift together the flour and a pinch of salt into a large bowl and stir in the apricots, figs and oats. Pour in the butter and sugar mixture and mix to form a dough. If it is too stiff, add a little milk.

Divide the dough into 24 pieces and roll each piece into a ball. Place 12 balls on each prepared baking sheet, spaced well apart, and press flat to a diameter of 6 cm/2½ inches. Mix the sultanas and walnuts together and press into the cookies.

Bake in the preheated oven for 15 minutes. Leave to cool on the baking sheets.

variation
top the cookies with
100 g/3½ oz mixed nuts
before baking

Peach, Pear & Plum Cookies

Makes about 30

225 g/8 oz butter, softened

140 g/5 oz caster sugar

1 egg yolk, lightly beaten

2 tsp almond extract

280 g/10 oz plain flour

pinch of salt

55 g/2 oz ready-to-eat dried
   peach, finely chopped

55 g/2 oz ready-to-eat dried
   pear, finely chopped

4 tbsp plum jam

Preheat the oven to 190°C/375°F/Gas Mark 5. Line two baking sheets with baking paper.

Put the butter and sugar into a bowl and mix well with a wooden spoon, then beat in the egg yolk and almond extract. Sift together the flour and a pinch of salt into the mixture, add the dried fruit and stir until thoroughly combined.

Scoop up tablespoons of the mixture, roll them into balls and place on the prepared baking sheets, spaced well apart. Make a hollow in the centre of each with the dampened handle of a wooden spoon. Fill the hollows with the jam.

Bake in the preheated oven for 12–15 minutes, until light golden brown. Leave to cool on the baking sheets for 5–10 minutes, then, using a palette knife, carefully transfer to wire racks to cool completely.

Peanut Partners

Makes about 30
225 g/8 oz butter, softened
140 g/5 oz caster sugar
1 egg yolk, lightly beaten
280 g/10 oz plain flour
1 tsp ground ginger
pinch of salt
2 tsp finely grated lemon rind

To decorate
3 tbsp smooth peanut butter
3 tbsp icing sugar
whole or chopped roasted peanuts

Put the butter and caster sugar into a bowl and mix well with a wooden spoon, then beat in the egg yolk. Sift together the flour, ginger and a pinch of salt into the mixture, add the lemon rind and stir until thoroughly combined. Halve the dough, shape into balls, wrap in clingfilm and chill in the refrigerator for 30–60 minutes.

Preheat the oven to 190°C/375°F/Gas Mark 5. Line two baking sheets with baking paper.

Unwrap the dough and roll out between two sheets of baking paper to about 3 mm/⅛ inch thick. Stamp out rounds with a 6-cm/2½-inch fluted cutter and put them on the prepared baking sheets, spaced well apart.

Bake in the preheated oven for 10–15 minutes, until golden brown. Leave to cool on the baking sheets for 5–10 minutes, then, using a palette knife, carefully transfer the cookies to wire racks to cool completely.

Beat together the peanut butter and icing sugar in a bowl, adding a little water if necessary. Spread the cookies with the peanut butter mixture and decorate with whole or chopped peanuts.

Something Special

Chocolate & Ginger Chequerboard Cookies

Makes 30

225 g/8 oz butter, softened

140 g/5 oz caster sugar

1 egg yolk, lightly beaten

2 tsp vanilla extract

280 g/10 oz plain flour

pinch of salt

1 tsp ground ginger

1 tbsp finely grated orange rind

1 tbsp cocoa powder, sifted

1 egg white, lightly beaten

Put the butter and sugar into a bowl and mix well with a wooden spoon, then beat in the egg yolk and vanilla extract. Sift together the flour and a pinch of salt into the mixture and stir until thoroughly combined.

Divide the dough in half. Add the ginger and orange rind to one half and mix well. Shape the dough into a log 15 cm/6 inch long. Flatten the sides and top to square off the log to 5 cm/2 inch high. Wrap in clingfilm and chill in the refrigerator for 30–60 minutes. Add the cocoa to the other half of the dough and mix well. Shape into a flattened log exactly like the first one, wrap in clingfilm and chill for 30–60 minutes.

Unwrap the dough and cut each log lengthways into three slices. Cut each slice lengthways into three strips. Brush the strips with egg white and stack them in threes, alternating the flavours, to make the log shapes again. Wrap in clingfilm and chill for 30–60 minutes. Preheat the oven to 190°C/375°F/Gas Mark 5. Line two baking sheets with baking paper. Unwrap the logs and cut into slices with a sharp serrated knife. Put the cookies on the sheets, spaced well apart. Bake for 12–15 minutes, until firm. Leave to cool for 5–10 minutes, then transfer to wire racks to cool.

Neapolitan Cookies

Makes 20

225 g/8 oz butter, softened
140 g/5 oz caster sugar
1 egg yolk, lightly beaten
1 tsp vanilla extract
300 g/10½ oz plain flour
salt
1 tbsp cocoa powder
½ tsp almond extract
few drops of green food
    colouring
1 egg white, lightly beaten

Put the butter and sugar into a bowl and mix well with a wooden spoon, then beat in the egg yolk. Divide the mixture equally among three bowls.

Beat the vanilla extract into the first bowl. Sift together one-third of the flour and a pinch of salt into the mixture and stir until combined. Shape into a ball, wrap in clingfilm and chill in the refrigerator for 30–60 minutes. Sift together one-third of the flour, the cocoa powder and a pinch of salt into the second bowl and stir. Shape into a ball, wrap in clingfilm and chill. Beat the almond extract into the third bowl. Sift together the flour and a pinch of salt and stir. Mix in green food colouring, then form into a ball, wrap in clingfilm and chill. Preheat the oven to 190°C/375°F/Gas Mark 5. Line two baking sheets with baking paper.

Roll out each piece of dough between two sheets of baking paper to rectangles. Brush the top of the vanilla dough with egg white and place the chocolate rectangle on top. Brush this with beaten egg white and place the almond rectangle on top. Using a sharp knife, cut into 5 mm/¼ inch thick slices, then cut each slice in half. Place on the prepared baking sheets and bake for 10–12 minutes. Leave to cool for 5–10 minutes, then transfer to wire racks to cool.

Cappuccino Cookies

Makes 30

2 sachets instant cappuccino
1 tbsp hot water
225 g/8 oz butter, softened
140 g/5 oz caster sugar
1 egg yolk, lightly beaten
280 g/10 oz plain flour
pinch of salt

To decorate

175 g/6 oz white chocolate,
    broken into pieces
cocoa powder, for dusting

Empty the cappuccino sachets into a small bowl and stir in the hot, but not boiling, water to make a paste. Put the butter and sugar into a bowl and mix well with a wooden spoon, then beat in the egg yolk and cappuccino paste. Sift together the flour and a pinch of salt into the mixture and stir until thoroughly combined. Halve the dough, shape into balls, wrap in clingfilm and chill in the refrigerator for 30–60 minutes.

Preheat the oven to 190°C/375°F/Gas Mark 5. Line two baking sheets with baking paper. Unwrap the dough and roll out between two sheets of baking paper. Stamp out cookies with a 6-cm/2½-inch round cutter and put them on the prepared baking sheets, spaced well apart.

Bake in the preheated oven for 10–12 minutes, until golden brown. Leave to cool for 5-10 minutes, then transfer to wire racks to cool. When the cookies are cool, place the wire racks over a sheet of baking paper. Put the chocolate into a heatproof bowl and melt over a pan of gently simmering water. Remove the bowl from the heat and leave to cool, then spoon the chocolate over the cookies. Gently tap the wire racks to level the surface and leave to set. Dust lightly with cocoa powder.

Spanish Almond Cookies

Makes 15

75 g/2¾ oz unsalted butter, softened, plus extra for greasing

55 g/2 oz blanched almonds

75 g/2¾ oz caster sugar

¼ tsp almond extract

55 g/2 oz plain flour

2 large egg whites

Preheat the oven to 180°C/350°F/Gas Mark 4. Grease several large baking sheets with butter.

Finely chop the almonds. Place the butter and sugar in a large bowl and beat together until light and fluffy. Add the almond extract, flour and chopped almonds and stir together until incorporated.

Place the egg whites in a large bowl and whisk until soft peaks form and they hold their shape but are not dry. Fold the egg whites into the almond mixture, then place 15 teaspoonfuls of the mixture on the prepared baking sheets, spaced well apart.

Bake in the preheated oven for 15–20 minutes, or until lightly golden brown around the edges. Leave to cool slightly on the baking sheets for 2–3 minutes, then transfer the cookies to a wire rack to cool completely.

variation
spoon melted chocolate over the cooled cookies and leave to set

Marshmallow Daisies

Makes 30
225 g/8 oz butter, softened
140 g/5 oz caster sugar
1 egg yolk, lightly beaten
2 tsp vanilla extract
225 g/8 oz plain flour
55 g/2 oz cocoa powder
pinch of salt

To decorate
about 90 white mini
   marshmallows, halved
   horizontally
4 tbsp peach jam
4 tbsp yellow sugar sprinkles

Put the butter and sugar into a bowl and mix well with a wooden spoon, then beat in the egg yolk and vanilla extract. Sift together the flour, cocoa powder and a pinch of salt into the mixture and stir until thoroughly combined. Halve the dough, roll each piece into a ball, wrap in clingfilm and chill in the refrigerator for 30–60 minutes.

Preheat the oven to 190°C/375°F/Gas Mark 5. Line two baking sheets with baking paper. Unwrap the dough and roll out between two sheets of baking paper to about 1 cm/½ inch thick and stamp out about 30 cookies with a 5-cm/2-inch flower cutter. Put them on the prepared baking sheets, spaced well apart.

Bake in the preheated oven for 10–12 minutes, until firm. Remove the baking sheets from the oven but do not turn off the heat. Arrange the pieces of marshmallow over the petals of the flowers, cutting them to fit if necessary. Return to the oven for 30–60 seconds, until the marshmallow has softened. Leave to cool on the baking sheets for 5–10 minutes, then transfer to wire racks to cool. Meanwhile, heat the jam in a small saucepan, strain into a bowl and leave to cool. Pipe a small circle of jam in the centre of each flower and top with the sugar sprinkles.

Thumbprint Cookies

Makes 36

115 g/4 oz unsalted butter,
    softened
125 g/4½ oz caster sugar
1 large egg, separated
1 tsp vanilla extract
175 g/6 oz plain flour
pinch of salt
25 g/1 oz ground almonds
100 g/3½ oz seedless
    raspberry jam

Preheat the oven to 180°C/350°F/Gas Mark 4. Line two large baking sheets with baking paper. Place the butter and 100 g/3½ oz of the sugar in a large bowl and beat together until light and fluffy. Add the egg yolk and vanilla extract and beat well to combine. Sift in the flour and a pinch of salt and mix well.

Mix the remaining sugar and the ground almonds together and spread out on a plate. Lightly whisk the egg white in a separate bowl. Roll walnut-sized pieces of dough into balls, then dip each ball into the egg white and roll in the almond sugar. Place the balls on the prepared baking sheets, spaced well apart, and make a deep indentation in each cookie.

Bake in the preheated oven for 10 minutes. Remove from the oven, press down again on each indentation and fill it with jam. Bake for a further 10–12 minutes or until the cookies are golden brown, turning the baking sheets once. Transfer to a wire rack and leave to cool.

Black & White Cookies

Makes 20

115 g/4 oz unsalted butter, plus extra for greasing

1 tsp vanilla extract

175 g/6 oz caster sugar

2 eggs, beaten

300 g/10½ oz plain flour

½ tsp baking powder

200 ml/7 fl oz milk

Icing

225 g/8 oz icing sugar

125 ml/4 fl oz double cream

⅛ tsp vanilla extract

75 g/2¾ oz plain chocolate, broken into pieces

Preheat the oven to 190°C/375°F/Gas Mark 5. Lightly grease three baking sheets with butter.

Place the butter, vanilla extract and caster sugar in a large bowl. Beat the mixture with a whisk until light and fluffy and then beat in the eggs one at a time.

Sift the flour and baking powder into the bowl and fold into the mixture, loosening with milk as you go until both are used up and the mixture is of dropping consistency.

Drop heaped tablespoonfuls of the mixture, spaced well apart, on the prepared baking sheets. Bake in the preheated oven for 15 minutes, until turning golden at the edges and light to the touch. Transfer to wire racks and leave to cool completely.

To make the icing, put the icing sugar in bowl and mix in half the cream and the vanilla extract. The consistency should be thick but spreadable. Using a small palette knife, spread half of each cookie with white icing. Now, melt the chocolate in a bowl set over a pan of simmering water. Remove from the heat and stir in the remaining cream. Spread the dark icing over the uncoated cookie halves. Leave to set.

Chinese Fortune Cookies

Makes 12

1–2 tbsp groundnut oil,
    for greasing

2 large egg whites

½ tsp vanilla extract

3 tbsp vegetable oil

100 g/3½ oz plain flour

1½ tsp cornflour

pinch of salt

150 g/5½ oz caster sugar

3 tsp water

Write fortune messages on thin strips of paper. Preheat the oven to 180°C/350°F/Gas Mark 4 and grease two large baking sheets with a little groundnut oil (do not preheat). Place the egg whites, vanilla extract and vegetable oil in a large bowl, then, using an electric whisk, beat together for 1 minute until frothy but not stiff.

Sift the flour, cornflour, a pinch of salt and sugar into a large bowl, stir in the water and mix. Add the egg white mixture and whisk until smooth. Make the cookies in batches of two by spooning 1 scant tablespoon of batter onto each half of the prepared baking sheet and tilting the baking sheet until the batter circles measure 8 cm/3 inches. Bake in the preheated oven for 7–8 minutes, until the edges are beginning to brown.

Work quickly to shape the cookies while still hot. Remove a cookie from the baking sheet with a spatula and fold the cookie in half to form a semi-circle. Pinch together at the top and fold the cookie over the rim of a cup. Then insert an index finger into each open end: bring your thumbs together to press into the middle to form the shape of the fortune cookie. Thread through the strip of paper and place on kitchen paper to cool. Repeat until all the batter is used.

Traditional Easter Cookies

Makes 30

225 g/8 oz butter, softened

140 g/5 oz caster sugar, plus extra for sprinkling

1 egg yolk, lightly beaten

280 g/10 oz plain flour

1 tsp mixed spice

pinch of salt

1 tbsp mixed peel

55 g/2 oz currants

1 egg white, lightly beaten

Place the butter and sugar in a large bowl and beat together until light and fluffy, then beat in the egg yolk. Sift together the flour, mixed spice and a pinch of salt into the mixture, add the mixed peel and currants and stir until thoroughly combined. Halve the dough, shape into balls, wrap in clingfilm and chill in the refrigerator for 30–60 minutes.

Preheat the oven to 190°C/375°F/Gas Mark 5. Line two large baking sheets with baking paper.

Unwrap the dough and roll out between two sheets of baking paper. Cut out cookies with a 6-cm/2½-inch fluted round cutter and place them on the prepared baking sheets, spaced well apart.

Bake in the preheated oven for 7 minutes, then brush with the egg white and sprinkle with the sugar. Bake for a further 5–8 minutes, or until light golden brown. Leave to cool on the baking sheets for 5–10 minutes, then transfer to wire racks to cool completely.

Turkish Delight Cookies

Makes 30

225 g/8 oz butter, softened

140 g/5 oz rose petal flavoured
  caster sugar

1 egg yolk, lightly beaten

1 tsp almond extract

280 g/10 oz plain flour

pinch of salt

100 g/3½ oz pistachio nuts,
  chopped

To decorate

175 g/6 oz white mini
  marshmallows, halved
  horizontally

25–55 g/1–2 oz desiccated
  coconut

Put the butter and sugar into a bowl and mix well with a wooden spoon, then beat in the egg yolk and almond extract. Sift together the flour and a pinch of salt into the mixture, add the pistachios and stir until thoroughly combined. Halve the dough, shape into balls, wrap in clingfilm and chill for 30–60 minutes.

Preheat the oven to 190°C/375°F/Gas Mark 5. Line two baking sheets with baking paper.

Unwrap the dough and roll out between two sheets of baking paper. Stamp out 6-cm/ 2½-inch squares and put them on the prepared baking sheets, spaced well apart.

Bake in the preheated oven for 12–15 minutes, until light golden brown, then remove from the oven. Cover the tops of the cookies with halved mini marshmallows. Brush with water and sprinkle with the coconut. Return to the oven for about 30 seconds, until the marshmallows have softened. Leave to cool on the baking sheets for 5–10 minutes, then, using a palette knife, transfer the cookies to wire racks to cool completely.

Lavender Cookies

Makes 40

225 g/8 oz butter, softened

175 g/6 oz caster sugar

1 large egg, lightly beaten

250 g/9 oz plain flour

2 tsp baking powder

1 tbsp dried lavender, chopped

Preheat the oven to 190°C/375°F/Gas Mark 5. Line two baking sheets with baking paper.

Put the butter and sugar into a bowl and mix well with a wooden spoon, then beat in the egg. Sift together the flour and baking powder into the mixture, add the lavender and stir until thoroughly combined.

Put tablespoons of the mixture on the prepared baking sheets, spaced well apart. Bake in the preheated oven for 15 minutes, until golden brown. Leave to cool on the baking sheets for 5–10 minutes, then, using a palette knife, carefully transfer to wire racks to cool completely.

variation
replace lavender with 1½ tsp of chopped dried rosemary

Sugar Cookie Hearts

Makes 30

225 g/8 oz butter, softened
280 g/10 oz caster sugar
1 egg yolk, lightly beaten
2 tsp vanilla extract
250 g/9 oz plain flour
25 g/1 oz cocoa powder
pinch of salt

To decorate

3–4 food colouring pastes
100 g/3½ oz plain chocolate,
  broken into pieces

Put the butter and half the sugar into a bowl and mix well with a wooden spoon, then beat in the egg yolk and vanilla extract. Sift together the flour, cocoa powder and a pinch of salt into the mixture and stir until thoroughly combined. Halve the dough, shape into balls, wrap in clingfilm and chill in the refrigerator for 30–60 minutes.

Preheat the oven to 190°C/375°F/Gas Mark 5. Line two baking sheets with baking paper. Unwrap the dough and roll out between two sheets of baking paper. Stamp out cookies with a heart-shaped cutter and put them on the prepared baking sheets, spaced well apart.

Bake in the preheated oven for 10–15 minutes, until firm. Leave to cool on the baking sheets for 5–10 minutes, then, using a palette knife, carefully transfer to wire racks to cool. Meanwhile, divide the remaining sugar among four small plastic bags or bowls. Add a little food colouring paste to each and rub in until well mixed. (Wear a plastic glove to prevent staining.) Put the chocolate in a heatproof bowl and melt over a pan of simmering water. Remove from the heat and leave to cool slightly. Spread the melted chocolate over the cookies on the racks and sprinkle with the coloured sugar. Leave to set.

Chocolate Dominoes

Makes 28

225 g/8 oz butter, softened

140 g/5 oz caster sugar

1 egg yolk, lightly beaten

2 tsp vanilla extract

250 g/9 oz plain flour

25 g/1 oz cocoa powder

pinch of salt

25 g/1 oz desiccated coconut

50 g/1¾ oz white chocolate chips

Put the butter and sugar into a bowl and mix well with a wooden spoon, then beat in the egg yolk and vanilla extract. Sift together the flour, cocoa powder and a pinch of salt into the mixture, add the coconut and stir until thoroughly combined. Halve the dough, shape into balls, wrap in clingfilm and chill in the refrigerator for 30–60 minutes.

Preheat the oven to 190°C/375°F/Gas Mark 5. Line two baking sheets with baking paper.

Unwrap the dough and roll out between two sheets of baking paper. Stamp out cookies with a 9-cm/3½-inch plain square cutter, then cut them in half to make rectangles. Put them on the prepared baking sheets, spaced well apart, and using a knife, make a line across the centre of each without cutting through. Arrange the chocolate chips on top of the cookies to look like dominoes, pressing them in gently.

Bake in the preheated oven for 10–15 minutes, until golden brown. Leave to cool on the baking sheets for 5–10 minutes, then, using a palette knife, carefully transfer to wire racks to cool completely.

Pear & Pistachio Cookies

Makes 30

225 g/8 oz butter, softened

140 g/5 oz caster sugar

1 egg yolk, lightly beaten

2 tsp vanilla extract

280 g/10 oz plain flour

pinch of salt

55 g/2 oz ready-to-eat dried pears, finely chopped

55 g/2 oz pistachio nuts, chopped

whole pistachio nuts, to decorate

Preheat the oven to 190°C/375°F/Gas Mark 5. Line two baking sheets with baking paper.

Put the butter and sugar into a bowl and mix well with a wooden spoon, then beat in the egg yolk and vanilla extract. Sift together the flour and a pinch of salt into the mixture, add the pears and pistachios and stir until thoroughly combined.

Scoop up tablespoons of the mixture and roll into balls. Put them on the prepared baking sheets, spaced well apart, and flatten slightly. Gently press a whole pistachio nut into the centre of each cookie.

Bake in the preheated oven for 10–15 minutes, until golden brown. Leave to cool on the baking sheets for 5–10 minutes, then, using a palette knife, carefully transfer to wire racks to cool completely.

variation
replace pistachios with chopped walnuts

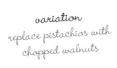

Carrot Cake Cookies

Makes 30

115 g/4 oz butter, softened

85 g/3 oz caster sugar

75 g/2¾ oz soft light brown sugar

1 large egg

½ tsp vanilla extract

150 g/5½ oz plain flour

½ tsp bicarbonate of soda

½ tsp ground cinnamon

85 g/3 oz carrots, finely grated

25 g/1 oz walnut halves, chopped

25 g/1 oz desiccated coconut

Preheat the oven to 190°C/375°F/Gas Mark 5. Line several large baking sheets with baking paper.

Place the butter and sugars in a large bowl and whisk together until pale and creamy. Whisk the egg and vanilla extract into the mixture until smooth. Sift in the flour, bicarbonate of soda and cinnamon, then beat together until well mixed. Add the grated carrot, chopped walnuts and coconut to the mixture and mix well together.

Drop heaped teaspoonfuls of the mixture on the prepared baking sheets, spaced well apart. Bake in the preheated oven for 8–10 minutes, or until lightly golden brown around the edges.

Leave to cool on the baking sheets for 2–3 minutes, then transfer to a wire rack to cool completely.

variation
spoon melted chocolate or
carob over the baked cookies

German Lebkuchen

Makes 60

3 eggs

200 g/7 oz caster sugar

55 g/2 oz plain flour

2 tsp cocoa powder

1 tsp ground cinnamon

½ tsp ground cardamom

¼ tsp ground cloves

¼ tsp ground nutmeg

175 g/6 oz ground almonds

55 g/2 oz mixed peel, finely
    chopped

To decorate

115 g/4 oz plain chocolate, broken
    into pieces

115 g/4 oz white chocolate, broken
    into pieces

sugar crystals

Preheat the oven to 180°C/350°F/Gas Mark 4. Line several large baking sheets with baking paper. Place the eggs and sugar in a heatproof bowl set over a saucepan of gently simmering water and whisk until thick and foamy. Remove the bowl from the pan and continue to whisk for 2 minutes.

Sift the flour, cocoa, cinnamon, cardamom, cloves and nutmeg into the bowl and stir in with the ground almonds and mixed peel. Drop heaped teaspoonfuls of the mixture on the prepared baking sheets, spreading them gently into smooth mounds.

Bake in the preheated oven for 15–20 minutes, or until light brown and slightly soft to the touch. Leave to cool on the baking sheets for 10 minutes, then transfer the cookies to wire racks to cool completely.

Place the plain and white chocolate in two separate heatproof bowls, set the bowls over two pans of gently simmering water and heat until melted. Dip half the biscuits in the melted plain chocolate and half in the white chocolate. Sprinkle with sugar crystals and leave to set.

Peach Daiquiri Cookies

Makes 30

225 g/8 oz butter, softened

140 g/5 oz caster sugar

finely grated rind of 1 lime

1 egg yolk, lightly beaten

2 tsp white rum

280 g/10 oz plain flour

100 g/3½ oz ready-to-eat dried peach, chopped

pinch of salt

To decorate

140 g/5 oz icing sugar

2 tbsp white rum

Preheat the oven to 190°C/375°F/Gas Mark 5. Line two baking sheets with baking paper.

Put the butter, caster sugar and lime rind into a bowl and mix well with a wooden spoon, then beat in the egg yolk and rum. Sift in the flour and a pinch of salt into the mixture, add the peach and stir until thoroughly combined.

Scoop up tablespoons of the dough and put them on the prepared baking sheets, spaced well apart, then flatten gently. Bake in the preheated oven for 10–15 minutes, until light golden brown. Leave to cool on the baking sheets for 5–10 minutes, then, using a palette knife, carefully transfer to wire racks to cool completely.

Sift the icing sugar into a bowl and stir in sufficient rum to give the mixture the consistency of thick cream. Leave the cookies on the racks and drizzle the icing over them with a teaspoon. Leave to set.

Double Heart Cookies

Makes 30

1 sachet instant latte

1½ tsp hot water

225 g/8 oz butter, softened

140 g/5 oz caster sugar

1 egg yolk, lightly beaten

250 g/9 oz plain flour

salt

1 tsp vanilla extract

3 tbsp cocoa powder

Put the instant latte into a small bowl and stir in the hot water to make a paste. Put the butter and sugar into a bowl and mix well with a wooden spoon, then beat in the egg yolk. Divide the mixture in half. Beat the latte paste into one half. Sift 140 g/5 oz of the flour with a pinch of salt into the mixture and stir. Shape the dough into a ball, wrap in clingfilm and chill in the refrigerator for 30–60 minutes.

Beat the vanilla extract into the other half, then sift together the remaining flour, the cocoa powder and a pinch of salt into the mixture and stir. Shape the dough into a ball, wrap in clingfilm and chill as above. Preheat the oven to 190°C/375°F/Gas Mark 5. Line two baking sheets with baking paper.

Unwrap both doughs and roll out each between two sheets of baking paper. Stamp out cookies with a 7-cm/2¾-inch heart-shaped cutter and put them on the prepared baking sheets, spaced well apart. Using a 4–5-cm/1½–2-inch heart-shaped cutter, stamp out the centres of each larger heart and remove from sheets. Put a small chocolate-flavoured heart in the centre of each large coffee-flavoured heart and vice versa. Bake for 10–15 minutes. Leave to cool for 5–10 minutes, then transfer to wire racks to cool completely.

Chocolate, Date & Pecan Nut Pinwheels

Makes 30

225 g/8 oz butter, softened

200 g/7 oz caster sugar

1 egg yolk, lightly beaten

225 g/8 oz plain flour

55 g/2 oz cocoa powder

pinch of salt

100 g/3½ oz pecan nuts,
   finely ground

280 g/10 oz dried dates,
   roughly chopped

finely grated rind of 1 orange

175 ml/6 fl oz orange
   flower water

Put the butter and 140 g/5 oz of the sugar into a bowl and mix well with a wooden spoon, then beat in the egg yolk. Sift together the flour, cocoa powder and a pinch of salt into the mixture, add the pecan nuts and stir until thoroughly combined. Halve the dough, shape into balls, wrap in clingfilm and chill for 30–60 minutes.

Put the dried dates, orange rind, orange flower water and remaining sugar into a saucepan and cook over a low heat, stirring constantly, until the sugar has dissolved. Bring to the boil, then lower the heat and simmer for 5 minutes. Remove the pan from the heat, pour the mixture into a bowl and leave to cool, then chill in the refrigerator.

Unwrap the dough and roll out between two pieces of baking paper to rectangles about 5 mm/¼ inch thick. Spread the date filling over the rectangles. Roll up the dough like a Swiss roll, wrap in the baking paper and chill for a further 30 minutes. Preheat the oven to 190°C/375°F/Gas Mark 5. Line two baking sheets with baking paper. Unwrap the rolls and cut into 1-cm/½ -inch slices. Put them on the sheets and bake for 15–20 minutes, until golden brown. Leave to cool on the sheets for 5–10 minutes, then transfer to wire racks to cool.

Margarita Cookies

Makes 30

225 g/8 oz butter, softened

140 g/5 oz caster sugar

finely grated rind of 1 lime

1 egg yolk, lightly beaten

2 tsp orange liqueur or 1 tsp
orange extract

280 g/10 oz plain flour

pinch of salt

To decorate

140 g/5 oz icing sugar

2 tbsp white tequila

Preheat the oven to 190°C/375°F/Gas Mark 5. Line two baking sheets with baking paper.

Put the butter, caster sugar and lime rind into a bowl and mix well with a wooden spoon, then beat in the egg yolk and orange liqueur or orange extract. Sift together the flour and a pinch of salt into the mixture and stir until thoroughly combined.

Scoop up tablespoons of the dough and put them on the prepared baking sheets, spaced well apart, then flatten gently. Bake in the preheated oven for 10–15 minutes, until light golden brown. Leave to cool on the baking sheets for 5–10 minutes, then, using a palette knife, carefully transfer to wire racks to cool completely.

Sift the icing sugar into a bowl and stir in sufficient tequila to give the mixture the consistency of thick cream. Leave the cookies on the racks and drizzle the icing over them with a teaspoon. Leave to set.

almonds
  Almond Cookies with a
    Cherry on Top 100
  Almond Crunchies 36
  Chocolate & Almond
    Biscotti 86
  Chocolate & Apricot
    Cookies 72
  German Lebkuchen 166
  Mini Florentines 32
  Spanish Almond Cookies 142
  Thumbprint Cookies 146
apples
  Apple Spice Cookies 102
  Mixed Fruit Cookies 42
apricots
  Chocolate & Apricot
    Cookies 72
  Crunchy Muesli Cookies 128

bananas
  Banana & Caramel
    Cookies 118
  Banana & Raisin Cookies 98
  Chocolate & Banana
    Cookies 84
Biscotti 40
Black & White Cookies 148
Blueberry & Cranberry
  Cinnamon Cookies 106
Brazil nuts: White Chocolate
  Cookies 14
Butter Cookies 44

Cappuccino Cookies 140
caramels
  Banana & Caramel
    Cookies 118
  Cinnamon & Caramel
    Cookies 30
Carrot Cake Cookies 164
cherries
  Almond Cookies with a
    Cherry on Top 100
  Chewy Candied Fruit
    Cookies 120
  Chocolate Mint Cookie
    Sandwiches 58
  Double Chocolate Cookies 28
  Iced Cherry Rings 116
  Mini Florentines 32
Chinese Fortune Cookies 150
chocolate
  Black & White Cookies 148
  Cappuccino Cookies 140
  Chocolate & Almond
    Biscotti 86
  Chocolate & Apricot
    Cookies 72
  Chocolate & Banana
    Cookies 84
  Chocolate & Coffee
    Wholemeal Cookies 82
  Chocolate & Ginger
    Chequerboard Cookies 136
  Chocolate & Orange Cookie
    Sandwiches 60
  Chocolate Buttons 90
  Chocolate, Date & Pecan
    Nut Pinwheels 172
  Chocolate Dominoes 160
  Chocolate Fudge Squares 66
  Chocolate Mint Cookie
    Sandwiches 58

Chocolate Orange Cookies 48
Chocolate Party Cookies 76
Chocolate Spread &
  Hazelnut Drops 68
Chocolate Sprinkle Cookies 64
Chocolate Wholemeals 70
Choco Mint Stars 78
Cookies & Cream
  Sandwiches 24
Double Chocolate Cookies 28
Double Heart Cookies 170
German Lebkuchen 166
Giant Chocolate Chunk
  Cookies 80
Golden Hazelnut Cookies 108
Lemon & Lime Cookies 110
Marshmallow Daisies 144
Mega Chip Cookies 52
Midnight Cookies 56
Mini Florentines 32
Mocha Walnut Cookies 62
Neapolitan Cookies 138
Orange & Chocolate
  Fingers 88
Sticky Ginger Cookies 34
Sugar Cookie Hearts 158
White Chocolate & Plum
  Cookies 74
White Chocolate Cookies 14
coconut
  Carrot Cake Cookies 164
  Chocolate Dominoes 160
  Choco Mint Stars 78
  Coconut & Cranberry
    Cookies 94
  Mango, Coconut & Ginger
    Cookies 126
  Turkish Delight Cookies 154
coffee
  Cappuccino Cookies 140
  Chocolate & Coffee
    Wholemeal Cookies 82
  Double Heart Cookies 170
  Mocha Walnut Cookies 62
  Walnut & Coffee Cookies 96
Cookies & Cream
  Sandwiches 24
cranberries
  Blueberry & Cranberry
    Cinnamon Cookies 106
  Coconut & Cranberry
    Cookies 94
  Crunchy Muesli Cookies 128

dates: Chocolate, Date & Pecan
  Nut Pinwheels 172

Easter Cookies, Traditional 152

figs
  Crunchy Muesli Cookies 128
  Walnut & Fig Pinwheels 122

German Lebkuchen 166
ginger
  Banana & Caramel
    Cookies 118
  Chocolate & Ginger
    Chequerboard Cookies 136
  Gingernuts 26
  Mango, Coconut & Ginger
    Cookies 126
  Mini Florentines 32
  Orange & Chocolate
    Fingers 88

Peanut Partners 132
Sticky Ginger Cookies 34

hazelnuts
  Chocolate & Coffee
    Wholemeal Cookies 82
  Chocolate Spread &
    Hazelnut Drops 68
  Golden Hazelnut Cookies 108
  Oaty Raisin & Hazelnut
    Cookies 18
honey
  Crunchy Muesli Cookies 128
  Crunchy Nut & Honey
    Cookie Sandwiches 124

Jam Rings 38

Lavender Cookies 156
lemons
  Biscotti 40
  Iced Cherry Rings 116
  Lemon & Lime Cookies 110
  Orange & Lemon Cookies 112
  Peanut Partners 132
limes
  Lemon & Lime Cookies 110
  Margarita Cookies 174
  Peach Daiquiri Cookies 168

macadamia nuts
  Chewy Candied Fruit
    Cookies 120
  Crunchy Nut & Honey
    Cookie Sandwiches 124
  Mango, Coconut & Ginger
    Cookies 126
maple syrup
  Chewy Candied Fruit
    Cookies 120
  Pecan & Maple Cookies 104
Margarita Cookies 174
marshmallows
  Marshmallow Daisies 144
  Turkish Delight Cookies 154
Midnight Cookies 56
mint, mints
  Chocolate Mint Cookie
    Sandwiches 58
  Choco Mint Stars 78
  Walnut & Fig Pinwheels 122
mixed peel
  Chewy Candied Fruit
    Cookies 120
  German Lebkuchen 166
  Traditional Easter Cookies 152
Mocha Walnut Cookies 62

Neapolitan Cookies 138
nuts see almonds; Brazil nuts;
  macadamia nuts; peanut
  butter; pecan nuts;
  pistachio nuts; walnuts

oats, oatmeal
  Chocolate & Coffee
    Wholemeal Cookies 82
  Classic Oatmeal Cookies 12
  Crunchy Muesli Cookies 128
  Oaty Raisin & Hazelnut
    Cookies 18
oranges
  Banana & Raisin Cookies 98
  Chocolate & Ginger
    Chequerboard Cookies 136

Chocolate & Orange
  Cookie Sandwiches 60
Chocolate Chip & Cinnamon
  Cookies 54
Chocolate, Date & Pecan
  Nut Pinwheels 172
Chocolate Orange Cookies 48
Gingernuts 26
Margarita Cookies 174
Mixed Fruit Cookies 42
Oaty Raisin & Hazelnut
  Cookies 18
Orange & Chocolate
  Fingers 88
Orange & Lemon Cookies 112

peaches
  Chewy Candied Fruit
    Cookies 120
  Peach Daiquiri Cookies 168
  Peach, Pear & Plum
    Cookies 130
peanut butter
  Peanut Butter & Grape
    Jelly Cookies 114
  Peanut Butter Cookies 20
  Peanut Partners 132
pears
  Mixed Fruit Cookies 42
  Peach, Pear & Plum
    Cookies 130
  Pear & Pistachio Cookies 162
pecan nuts
  Chocolate, Date & Pecan Nut
    Pinwheels 172
  Pecan & Maple Cookies 104
pistachio nuts
  Biscotti 40
  Pear & Pistachio Cookies 162
  Turkish Delight Cookies 154
plums, prunes
  Mixed Fruit Cookies 42
  Peach, Pear & Plum
    Cookies 130
  White Chocolate & Plum
    Cookies 74

raisins, sultanas & currants
  Banana & Raisin Cookies 98
  Chocolate & Banana
    Cookies 84
  Crunchy Muesli Cookies 128
  Mini Florentines 32
  Oaty Raisin & Hazelnut
    Cookies 18
  Traditional Easter Cookies 152

Simple Cookies 16
Spanish Almond Cookies 142
Sugar Cookie Hearts 158

Thumbprint Cookies 146
Turkish Delight Cookies 154

walnuts
  Carrot Cake Cookies 164
  Crunchy Muesli Cookies 128
  Mocha Walnut Cookies 62
  Walnut & Coffee Cookies 96
  Walnut & Fig Pinwheels 122
wheatgerm
  Chocolate Wholemeals 70
  Healthy Wholemeal
    Cookies 46